THE TROJAN WAR
NEW EDITION

The
TROJAN WAR
New Edition

The Chronicles of Dictys of Crete
and Dares the Phrygian

TRANSLATED
WITH AN INTRODUCTION AND NOTES BY

R. M. FRAZER JR.

Indiana University Press

This book is a publication of

Indiana University Press
Office of Scholarly Publishing
Herman B Wells Library 350
1320 East 10th Street
Bloomington, Indiana 47405 USA

iupress.indiana.edu

First paperback edition 2019
© 1966 by Indiana University Press

Original 1966 Edition Library of Congress Catalog Card Number: 65-19709

ISBN 978-0-253-04342-9 <pbk>

1 2 3 4 5   23 22 21 20 19

CONTENTS

v

PREFACE

Dictys of Crete and Dares the Phrygian can tell us things about the Trojan War that Homer cannot because Homer did not live until long after the war's conclusion but Dictys and Dares were actually there. Dictys traveled to Troy with the Cretan army as part of the Greek alliance that assembled to retrieve Helen. Dares, on the other hand, fought to defend the city under the Trojan prince Antenor. Both recorded the events of the war—including its causes, its major battles, and its aftermath, as well as the actions of leaders on both sides—in simple, direct prose. While the real story of the Trojan War had been clouded, over the centuries, by competing accounts littered with historical inaccuracies and pure figments of imagination, Dictys and Dares finally provide us with authentic accounts and real eyewitness descriptions of the most famous and controversial event in ancient history. Or so they would have us believe.

While modern historical and archaeological research has concluded that a city in the Dardanelles was destroyed by sword and flame during the Bronze Age, perhaps by a Panhellenic alliance, neither Dictys of Crete nor Dares the Phrygian were there to see it. In fact, whoever authored these texts were almost definitely not named Dictys and Dares (though we refer to them as such), and they did not live until long after Homer had composed the *Iliad* and the *Odyssey*. Two papyrus fragments discovered in the early twentieth century have allowed scholars to identify a Greek version of Dictys that probably dates to the late first century A.D., sometime after the reign of Nero. The Latin version of Dictys's

text appears to have been produced during the fourth century
A.D. The Latin Dares, for which no Greek source has been found,
may have originated in the late fifth century following the sack of
Rome in 410. In the centuries after they first began to circulate,
some readers doubted the chronicles' validity while others treated
them as valuable historical records. These two texts eventually
came to be regarded as forgeries, and their authors as perpetrators
of an elaborate historiographical hoax. Some scholars and critics in the nineteenth and early twentieth centuries derided their
simple Latin prose style, but more recently the works of Dictys
and Dares have come to be recognized as important literary artifacts of the late antique era and foundational texts in the medieval
Trojan tradition.

The History of the Trojan War

The Trojan narratives of Dictys and Dares include prefaces
that help give context for the works and explain how these "eyewitness accounts" remained hidden for so long. Some copies of Dictys's account circulated with an anonymous preface claiming he
wrote a nine-volume history of the Trojan War in the Phoenician
alphabet based on his own experience. According to this preface,
the book was buried with Dictys on the island of Crete, remaining
hidden underground until an earthquake exposed the contents of
the grave. Dictys's book was then delivered to the Roman emperor Nero, who ordered it translated into Greek. Other manuscripts include a letter purportedly from a Roman called Lucius
Septimus, who presents a slightly different version of the book's
discovery and claims to be the translator of the Latin edition. It is
Lucius Septimus who refers to Dictys's text as the *Ephemeris belli
Troiani* (*Journal of the Trojan War*).

In a prefatory letter that opens Dares the Phrygian's *De excidio Troiae historia* (*The Fall of Troy, A History*), a writer claiming

to be first-century Roman biographer Cornelius Nepos says that he has faithfully translated this text, which had been "written in Dares' own hand," from Greek to Latin. Scholars have debated whether a Greek version of the *De excidio* ever really existed, and it is certain that the letter and translation were not authored by Cornelius Nepos. The letter asks the readers to decide whether to trust the accounts of Dares the Phrygian or Homer, noting that Dares participated in the Trojan War while Homer was not born until "long after the War was over." It goes on to point out that even the Athenians "found Homer insane for describing gods battling with mortals,"[1] suggesting that any discrepancies between Dares's and Homer's narratives, of which there are many, should be resolved by privileging Dares's firsthand *De excidio*.

Of course, even as they try to discredit Homer in order to establish their own authority, Dictys and Dares use the works of Homer and his literary progeny as the basis for their own texts. While Dictys likely had access to a Greek manuscript of the *Iliad*, Dares may have known Homer only through a Latin translation or summary. Around the beginning of the first millennium A.D., Homer was known directly by Greek audiences and some Romans, but he was mediated through a number of other writers who present additional or conflicting information about the Trojan War. Poems in the ancient Greek epic cycle, now only fragmentary, present the details of stories to which Homer only alludes, such as the building of the Trojan horse and the death of Odysseus after his return to Ithaca. Dramatists throughout the classical era staged various Homeric and counter-Homeric episodes from the Trojan War's origin, duration, and aftermath. For example, Herodotus claims that Helen never made it to Troy but was in Egypt during the war, and the tragedian Euripides uses the Egypt story as the basis for his *Helen*.

Dictys and Dares also seek to supplant Virgil, who had modeled his Trojan epic on Homer's *Iliad* and *Odyssey*. Composed in Latin verse toward the end of the first century B.C., Virgil's *Aeneid* narrates the efforts of the Trojan prince Aeneas to establish a Trojan settlement in Italy that will lead to the rise of imperial Rome. Both Dictys and Dares challenge the famed piety of Virgil's Aeneas by describing how he helps lead a plot to betray Troy to the Greeks, making him responsible for the destruction of the city. Virgil, like Homer, shows the gods playing an active role in human affairs, so his poetic fantasies, therefore, can be disregarded while the true narrative of the Trojan War can be found in Dictys and Dares's historical chronicles. Using simple prose and presenting the events as the result of human deliberation and action, Dictys and Dares inaugurate a new model for representing the Trojan War as the foundational moment of secular history.

Dictys and Dares

There are no gods in Dictys and Dares, only politics. We see the Trojans and Greeks meeting in council, engaging in diplomacy, and clashing on the battlefield with their own rhetorical and martial skills driving the action. The *Ephemeris* and the *De excidio* reflect the late antique world in which they were produced, a world shaped by the Roman Empire and the spread of Christianity. While perhaps influenced by a Christian perspective in their rejection of the old gods of Greek and Roman mythology, these texts can hardly be called Christian, as neither text recognizes any sort of divinity shaping the destinies of the people involved in the war. After the fifth century, the texts of Dictys and Dares circulated in a post-Roman world in which various territories around Europe were establishing new models of political power. For the audiences that read Dictys and Dares throughout late antiquity and the middle ages, the fall of Troy would be understood in the context of the fall of Rome.

Dictys's *Ephemeris* begins in Crete, where Agamemnon and Menelaus have traveled to claim their inheritance from Atreus.

With Menelaus away from Sparta, Alexander (also known as Paris) carries off Helen and her property, taking her back to Troy. When the Trojans refuse to return Helen, the Greeks assemble their armies. Writing as a soldier in the Cretan army that fights in support of Menelaus's cause, Dictys could be seen as favoring the Greek side as he condemns Paris for his "very foul crime" and "criminal lust" (Book One, section three; Book Five). Book One and the first part of Book Two detail the Greeks diplomatic efforts to recover Helen and the debates among the Trojan nobility regarding how to respond. The second half of Book Two and Book Three adapt the narrative of the *Iliad* with some notable changes, primarily as human actors replace the gods and Achilles's rage stems not from his grief for Patroclus but from his desire for the Trojan Polyxena, a daughter of Priam and sister of Hector. Books Three through Five describe the events leading up to the end of the war by adapting, amplifying, and sometimes confounding Trojan material from the classical tradition as the Trojans Antenor and Aeneas conspire with the Greeks to bring down Troy. Book Six presents the *nostoi*, the largely tragic accounts of the Greek heroes' return home.

Dares's *De excidio* is much shorter than Dictys's *Ephemeris*, even as it describes the first destruction of Troy by Jason and Hercules, which serves as a prequel and motive for the more famous Trojan War. Having been offended by the Trojans' refusal of hospitality, Hercules leads a Greek army against Troy, killing King Laomedon and carrying off Laomedon's daughter, and sister to Priam, Hesione. After Priam assumes the kingship, he rebuilds Troy and sends Antenor to ask the Greeks to return Hesione. When the Greeks refuse, Paris travels to Sparta, takes Helen back to Troy, and refuses to return her, despite Cassandra's warnings. As in Dictys, Antenor and Aeneas betray Troy to the Greeks, but rather than smuggling the Greek army into Troy in the Trojan horse, Dares says that Antenor and Aeneas let the Greek army into the city through the Scaean gate, "the one whose exterior was carved with a horse's head."[2] Dares's narrative ends just after the destruction of the city with Aeneas somewhat ominously sailing away from the fallen Troy. Though less comprehensive than Dictys's *Ephemeris*, Dares's *De excidio* would be the privileged account throughout the Middle Ages partially because of its pro-Trojan slant.

Readers familiar with the story of the Trojan War from Homer and Virgil's poems will be surprised by much of what they find in the accounts of Dictys and Dares. Familiar characters behave in unfamiliar ways, sometimes motivated by very different forces from what drives them in the classical tradition. The rivalry between Achilles and Hector plays out quite differently than it does in the *Iliad*, as Hector's sister Polyxena plays a significant role. The Trojan prince Troilus, mentioned only briefly in the *Iliad*, emerges as a prominent voice in Trojan parliament and a leader on the battlefield; he becomes a major character in the medieval tradition. Where Homer had provided a catalog of ships to describe the Greek fleet that sailed for Troy, Dares presents brief portraits of the Greek and Trojan dramatis personae. Although the chronicles of Dictys and Dares had been regarded by some critics as simple, somewhat strange narratives written in bad Latin, these texts have more recently been acknowledged for their literary significance as they reinvent the Trojan legend for a new age in European history.

The Medieval Tradition of Troy

Dictys and Dares provide the basis for the medieval tradition of Troy. Royal genealogies and chronicle histories constructed to legitimize European political dynasties in regions of France, Italy, Germany, and England claimed Troy as a site of ancestral origin. By establishing a Trojan lineage, these emerging European nation-states sought to define themselves as the next great imperial power after the fall of the Roman Empire. The medieval concept of *translatio studii et imperii* (the translation, or transfer, of learning and empire) promoted the notion that cultural and political hegemony that could be passed from one civilization to another in a continuous legacy that could be traced back to Troy through Rome. Virgil's *Aeneid* provides a literary model for representing the *translatio studii et imperii*, but medieval authors took their "historical" information about the fall of Troy from the chronicles of Dictys and Dares. The synthesis of these three texts generates some of the most important and influential literature of the European Middle Ages.

As European nations began to establish their own literary traditions in the vernacular, Benoît de Sainte-Maure translated and adapted the Latin chronicles into thirty thousand lines of Old French verse. Composed between 1155 and 1160, Benoît's *Le Roman de Troie* is one of the twelfth-century *romans d'antiquité* that presents stories from ancient history in the vernacular for a courtly audience (for example, *Le Roman de Thèbes* adapts Statius's *Thebaid* and the *Roman d'Eneas* retells and expands Virgil's *Aeneid*). These French romances medievalize their ancient sources, adding the narrative and emotional elements of what is now commonly referred to as "courtly love." At the start of *Le Roman de Troie*, Benoît echoes the prefaces to the *De excidio* as he writes that Dares, who was born in Troy, witnessed these events himself. Whether or not Benoît believed Dictys and Dares's claims of authenticity, their works lent authority to his own poem.

A little more than a century later, Guido delle Colonne translated Benoît's French poem into a Latin prose chronicle, the *Historia destructionis Troiae*. Completed in 1287, Guido's *Historia* returns the Trojan narrative to the language and form used by Dares and Dictys. Guido never acknowledges Benoît as his source, though he relies heavily on the *Roman de Troie*, but instead cites only Dictys and Dares. In his prologue, Guido says that

Homer, Virgil, and Ovid all mixed truth and fiction, and he claims that the first Latin translators of Dictys and Dares abridged their texts, but he promises that his *Historia* will present a true and comprehensive history, thus allowing his Latin chronicle to both preserve and supplement even the original "eyewitness" accounts of the Trojan War.

Guido's *Historia* would become the standard historical account of the Trojan War for the next few centuries. It was translated into Middle English during the late fourteenth century at least three times, serving as the base text for the *Laud Troy Book*, the *Gest Historyale*, and *The Seege of Troye*. In the early fifteenth century, John Lydgate translated Guido's *Historia* into Middle English poetry at the request of King Henry V (*Troy Book*, 1422). Raoul Lefèvre used the *Historia* for book 3 of his French prose *Recueil des histoires de Troyes* (1464), and this Trojan history would be translated and printed by William Caxton as the prose *Recuyell of the Historyes of Troye* (1474); this was the first book printed in English. These medieval Trojan narratives would be read alongside Virgil and Homer throughout the Renaissance, influencing works such as Edmund Spenser's epic poem *The Faerie Queene* (1596) and plays such as William Shakespeare's *Troilus and Cressida* (1602).

Dictys and Dares play an important role in English historiography and literature as England claims Trojan descent through Aeneas's grandson Brutus, who journeys from Italy to the island of Britain, where he settles with his Trojan army and establishes a city on the Thames as a New Troy. This foundational myth first appears in Geoffrey of Monmouth's *Historia regum Britanniae* (1136), which uses a framing device and Latin prose style similar to the *De excidio* and the *Ephemeris*. Manuscript copies of Geoffrey's *Historia*, which was rather popular in the Middle Ages, often circulated in collections that included copies of Dares. In the late twelfth century, Joseph of Exeter's *Ylias of Dares Phrygius* translated and adapted Dares and Dictys, as well as other sources, into Latin hexameters. At the end of the fourteenth century, Chaucer names Dares and Dictys as writers who help "bear up" the story of Troy in his *House of Fame* (Book II, lines 1464–72); he cites Dares in *The Book of the Duchess* (Book II, lines 1067–71) and his great Trojan poem, *Troilus and Criseyde* (Book V, lines 1765–71).

The narrative of the Trojan War established by Dictys and Dares and transmitted through their adaptations by Benoît and Guido delle Colonne inspired two of the most significant literary texts of the fourteenth century: Boccaccio's *Il Filostrato* (ca. 1340) and Chaucer's *Troilus and Criseyde* (ca. 1386). In his Italian poem, Boccaccio makes the Trojan War the background for the love affair between Troilo and Criseida, a romantic subplot first featured in the *Roman de Troie*. Chaucer translates and adapts *Il Filostrato* into Middle English in his *Troilus*, which would, in turn, influence the Trojan narratives of writers like Lydgate, Caxton, and Shakespeare. Through many translations and adaptations, the chronicles of Dares and Dictys helped shape English literature, historiography, and political discourse for one thousand years after they first appeared.

R. M. Frazer's Translation and Modern Scholarship

When R. M. Frazer's *The Trojan War: The Chronicles of Dictys of Crete and Dares the Phrygian* was published in 1966, the edition provided the first complete English translation of both texts. For his source texts, Frazer used Werner Eisenhut's *Dictys Cretensis Ephemeridos belli Troiani libri* (1958) and Ferdinand Meister's *Daretis Phrygii de excidio Troiae historia* (1873). In his review of the present translation, Gildas Roberts remarks that "Frazer's English flatters the wretched Latin of Dares."

In the late nineteenth century, German philologists published studies of the *De excidio* and the *Ephemeris*, but English-language critics puzzled over why Dares and Dictys ever received any attention at all. Describing Dares as an example of late antique literary fraud, Alfred Gudeman wrote in 1894 that the *De excidio* "stands without a rival in the ludicrous absurdity of its information and in the naïve credulity which its author presumes in its readers."[3] In one of the first major American studies of these texts, a dissertation published in 1906, Nathaniel Griffin acknowledged the popularity of Dares and Dictys in the Middle Ages despite their "total lack of intrinsic literary merit."[4] A few years later, Griffin brought to scholars' attention the discovery of a papyrus fragment that confirmed Dictys's text had originally been composed in Greek ("The Greek Dictys").

A begrudging acceptance of the importance of Dares and Dictys began to give way in the past fifty years to genuine interest. In a paper delivered to the Medieval Academy in 1964, Robert Lumiansky boldly argued for the literary merits of Dares and Dictys, claiming that Dares's *De excidio* is "a thoroughly effective narrative"[5] and that Dictys's "regular assessment of human behavior" in his moral commentary helped account for the popularity of *Ephemeris*. In the 1990s, Stefan Merkle published a series of essays that consider Dares and Dictys in their historical context. During this same period, Francis Ingledew and James Simpson published essays in *Speculum* that consider the classical and medieval modes of Trojan historiography. Barbara Nolan's *Chaucer and the Tradition of the "Roman Antique"* considers Benoît's adaptation of Dares and Dictys and its influence on Chaucer. Frederic Clark has written about Dares's reputation in medieval and early modern Europe. In light of the 2004 Hollywood blockbuster *Troy*, Jon Solomon traces the widely disparate accounts of the Trojan War from the classical era through the twentieth century.

R. M. Frazer's translation makes the Trojan narratives of Dares and Dictys accessible to English readers, allowing them to explore the inventiveness of these texts. Dares and Dictys participate in a long tradition of presenting elaborate fictions as the "truth" of the Trojan War, but their lack of authenticity should not diminish their value. Dictys and Dares reimagine the history of Troy in order to help a new generation make sense of their own place in history, and their works play a significant role in the development of national histories and literatures during the European Middle Ages and Renaissance. Recent scholarship in the classics, history, literature, and medieval studies has only begun to explore the intricacies and oddities of these unique textual artifacts. This translation will be a valuable tool for the continuing study and appreciation of Dictys and Dares, champions of the Trojan War.

Timothy D. Arner
Grinnell College

Notes

1. See in this book, page 133.

2. Ibid., 40

3. See Alfred Gudeman, "Literary Frauds among the Romans," *Transactions of the American Philological Association* 25 (1894): 152.

4. See Nathaniel E. Griffin, *Dares and Dictys: An Introduction to the Story of Medieval Versions of the Troy Story.* PhD diss., Johns Hopkins University (Baltimore, MD: Furst, 1906), 6.

5. See Robert M. Lumiansky, "Dares' *Historia* and Dictys' *Ephemeris*: A Critical Comment," in *Studies in Language, Literature, and Culture of the Middle Ages and Later*, ed. E. Bagby Atwood and Archibald A. Hill (Austin: University of Texas Press, 1969), 205.

Bibliography

Barnicle, M. E., ed. *The Seege or Batayle of Troye.* Early English Text Society Original Series 172. London: Oxford University Press, 1927.

Benoît de Saint-Maure. *Le Roman de Troie.* 6 vols. Edited by Léopold Constans. Paris: Firmin Didot, 1904–12.

Benoît de Sainte-Maure. *The Roman de Troie*. Translated by Glyn S. Burgess and Douglas Kelly. Cambridge, UK: D. S. Brewer, 2017.

Benson, C. David. *The History of Troy in Middle English Literature: Guido delle Colonne's Historia Destructionis Troiae in Medieval England.* Cambridge, UK: D. S. Brewer, 1980.

Boccaccio, Giovanni. *Il Filostrato*. Edited by Vincenzo Pernicone. Translated by Robert P. apRoberts and Anna Bruni Seldis. New York: Garland, 1986.

Bradley, Dennis R. "Troy Revisted." *Hermes* 119 (1991): 232–46.

Caxton, William. *The Recuyell of the Historyes of Troye*. Edited by Oskar Sommer. London: David Nutt, 1894.

Chaucer, Geoffrey. *The Riverside Chaucer*. 3rd ed. Boston: Houghton Mifflin, 1987.

Clark, Frederic. "Authenticity, Antiquity, and Authority: Dares Phrygius in Early Modern Europe." *Journal of the History of Ideas* 72 (2011): 183–207.

———. "Reading the 'First Pagan Historiographer': Dares Phrygius and Medieval Genealogy." *Viator* 41 (2010): 203–26.

Desmond, Marilyn. "Trojan Itineraries and the Matter of Troy." In *The Oxford History of Classical Reception in English Literature, Volume 1 (800–1558)*, edited by Rita Copeland, 251–68. Oxford: Oxford University Press, 2016.

Farrow, James G. "Aeneas and Rome: Pseudepigraphia and Politics." *Classical Journal* 87 (1992): 339–59.

Frazer, R. M. *The Trojan War: The Chronicles of Dictys of Crete and Dares the Phrygian*. Bloomington: Indiana University Press, 1966.

Griffin, Nathaniel E. *Dares and Dictys: An Introduction to the Story of Medieval Versions of the Troy Story*. PhD diss., Johns Hopkins University. Baltimore, MD: Furst, 1906.

———. "The Greek Dictys." *American Journal of Philology* 29 (1908): 329–35.

———. "Un-Homeric Elements in the Medieval Story of Troy." *Journal of English and Germanic Philology* 7 (1907–1908): 32–52.

Gudeman, Alfred. "Literary Frauds among the Romans." *Transactions of the American Philological Association* 25 (1894): 140–64.

Guido delle Colonne. *Historia destructionis Troiae*. Edited by Nathaniel Edward Griffin. Cambridge, MA: N.p., 1936.

———. *Historia destructionis Troiae*. Translated by Mary Elizabeth Meek. Bloomington: Indiana University Press, 1974.

Hansen, William. "Strategies of Authentication in Ancient Popular Literature." In *The Ancient Novel and Beyond*, edited by Stelios Panayotakis, Maaike Zimmerman, and Wytse Keulen, 301–14. Leiden: Brill, 2003.

Homer. *The Iliad*. Translated by Richmond Lattimore. Chicago: University of
     Chicago Press, 1951.

Ingledew, Francis. "The Book of Troy and the Genealogical Construction of
     History: The Case of Geoffrey of Monmouth's *Historia regum Britanniae*."
     Speculum 69 (1994): 665–704.

Joseph of Exeter. *The Iliad of Dares Phrygius*. Translated by A. G. Rigg.
     Toronto: Centre for Medieval Studies, 2005. http://medieval.utoronto. ca/ylias/

Lumiansky, Robert M. "Dares' *Historia* and Dictys' *Ephemeris*: A Critical
     Comment." In *Studies in Language, Literature, and Culture of the Middle
     Ages and Later*, edited by E. Bagby Atwood and Archibald A. Hill, 200–9.
     Austin: University of Texas Press, 1969.

Lydgate, John. *Troy Book*. 4 vols. Edited by Henry Bergen. Early English Text
     Society ES 97, 103,106, 126. London: Kegan Paul, Trench, Trubner & Co.,
     1906–35.

Merkle, Stefan. "News from the Past: Dictys and Dares on the Trojan War."
     In *Latin Fiction: The Latin Novel in Context*, edited by Heinz Hofmann,
     155–66. New York: Routledge, 1999.

———. "Telling the True Story of the Trojan War: The Eyewitness Account
     of Dictys of Crete." In *The Search for the Ancient Novel*, edited by James
     Tatum, 183–96. Baltimore, MD: Johns Hopkins University Press, 1994.

———. "The Truth and Nothing but the Truth: Dictys and Dares." In *The
     Novel in the Ancient World*, edited by Gareth Schmeling, 563–80. Leiden:
     Brill, 1996.

Nolan, Barbara. *Chaucer and the Tradition of the "Roman Antique."*
     Cambridge, UK: Cambridge University Press, 1992.

Panton, George A., and David Donaldson, eds. *The "Gest hystoriale" of the
     Destruction of Troy: An Alliterative Romance Translated from Guido de
     Colonna's "Hystoria Troiana."* Early English Text Society Original Series
     39, 56. London: N. Trübner, 1869–74.

Roberts, Gildas. "Review: *The Trojan War: The Chronicles of Dictys of Crete
     and Dares the Phrygian* by R. M. Frazer, Jr." *Classical Journal* 62 (1967):
     282.

Root, R. K. "Chaucer's Dares." *Modern Philology* 15 (1918): 1–22.

Shakespeare, William. *Troilus and Cressida*. The Arden Shakespeare, 3rd
     Series, rev. ed. Edited by David Bevington. London: Bloomsbury, 2015.

Simpson, James. "The Other Book of Troy: Guido delle Colonne's *Historia
     destructionis Troiae* in Fourteenth- and Fifteenth-Century England."
     Speculum 73 (1998): 397–423.

Solomon, Jon. "The Vacillations of the Trojan Myth: Popularization and Classicization, Variation and Codification." *International Journal of the Classical Tradition* 14 (2007): 482–534.

Spenser, Edmund. *The Faerie Queene.* Edited by A. C. Hamilton. 2nd rev. ed. Harlow: Pearson Longman, 2007.

Strohm, Paul. "Storie, Spelle, Geste, Romaunce, Tragedie: Generic Distinctions in the Middle English Troy Narratives." *Speculum* 46 (1971): 348–59.

Virgil. *Eclogues, Georgics, Aeneid.* Translated by H. R. Fairclough and G. P. Goold. Loeb Classical Library, vols. 63 and 64. Cambridge, MA: Harvard University Press. 1916, 1999.

Wulfing, J. Ernst, ed. *The Laud Troy Book.* Early English Text Society. London: Kegan Paul, Trench, Trubner & Co., 1902.

Editions

Eisenhut, Werner, ed. *Dictys Cretensis Ephemeridos belli Troiani libri: A Lucio Septimio ex Graeco in latinam sermonem translati; accidit papyrus Oictyis Graeci ad Tebtunium inventa.* Leipzig: Teubner, 1958.

Meister, Ferdinand Otto, ed. *Daretis Phrygii de excidio Troiae historia.* Leipzig: Teubner, 1873.

Acknowledgments

The present volume brings together for the first time in English translation the accounts of Dictys and Dares about the Trojan War. These works deserve our careful attention as the principal sources of the medieval Troy story and as examples of the anti-Homeric literature of late antiquity.

In the Introduction, I have briefly both described the influence of our authors on later European literature and tried to show how our Latin texts depend on Greek originals. For the latter purpose, I have found the scholarship of Nathaniel Edward Griffin especially rewarding for Dictys and that of Otmar Schissel von Fleschenberg for Dares. I have used the Notes to comment on matters of form (how our Latin texts probably differ from their Greek originals), to point out difficulties and inconsistencies, and to cite some of the sources and parallel versions of the stories that Dictys and Dares tell.

My grateful acknowledgment for kind advice and encouragement goes first to Graydon W. Regenos. Many thanks are also due to Robert M. Lumiansky, Sanford G. Etheridge, Gardner B. Taplin, Ronald E. White, and Robert P. Sonkowsky, all of whom gave me their help in various ways.

R. M. F.

THE TROJAN WAR
NEW EDITION

INTRODUCTION

The Medieval Troy Story

The works of Dictys and Dares are short prose narratives about the Trojan War. Though they were probably composed, in their original Greek forms, during the first century A.D., they claim to antedate Homer. Their authors are supposed to have actually fought at Troy and to have made first-hand reports of the War. The longer and fuller work is that of Dictys which alone of the two describes how the Greeks returned to their homelands.

Several writers of the Byzantine period based their accounts of the Trojan War on the original Dictys, but there is little traceable influence of Dares on later Greek literature. The reason for this is the fact that Dictys is written from the point of view of the Greeks, Dares from that of the Trojans.[1]

The Greek texts of both authors, with the exception of a small fragment of Dictys, have not survived. They were, however, during the early middle ages, translated, more or less completely, into Latin; and this is how we know them.

The Latin Dictys and Dares exercised a major influence on the medieval Troy story. But now Dares was more popular than Dictys, for the Latin-speaking West had inherited a pro-Trojan bias from the Romans, who claimed descent from the Trojans. About 1160 A.D. Benoit de Sainte-Maure based his *Le Roman de Troie* upon our authors. His main source was Dares, but he also used Dictys, especially toward the end of his work where the former authority failed him.

The most famous story contained in the *Roman* is that of

3

Troilus and Briseida, which Benoit himself presumably created
on the basis of a few disconnected passages in Dares. Dares' con-
tributions to the Troilus romance can be summarized as follows:[2]
First, he describes the appearance of the main characters—
Troilus, Briseida, and Diomedes.[3] Secondly, he relates that
Troilus, in one of his fights, wounds Diomedes.[4] And finally, he
reports that Calchas, the Trojan priest, meets Achilles at Delphi
and joins the Greeks at the command of the oracle.[5]

Benoit's poem found many translators and imitators, and
thus was largely responsible for spreading the accounts of Dictys
and Dares throughout Western Europe. The most influential of
Benoit's adapters was the thirteenth-century Sicilian judge Guido
delle Colonne, who wrote his *Historia Destructionis Troiae* in
Latin prose.[6] Guido cites Dictys and Dares as his sources and
never so much as mentions Benoit. Nevertheless, the *Historia* has
been proved to be, for the most part, an abridging paraphrase of
the *Roman*.[7] It offers a shortened and somewhat altered Troilus
and Briseida story.[8]

In the *Roman* (and therefore in the *Historia*) the Troilus
story must be pieced together from several different passages.
A unified version was first created by Boccaccio in his *Il Filostrato*
("The One Prostrated by Love"). Boccaccio's main source was
Benoit; he is probably indebted to Guido for only a few slight
touches.[9] The *Filostrato* expands the original version; it describes
how Troilo becomes enamored of Criseida (for thus the heroine
is renamed)[10] and how he wins her love, and it adds the character
of Pandaro.[11]

The description of Troilo's falling in love and the addition
of the go-between were undoubtedly influenced by another story
in the *Roman,* which told how Achilles fell under the spell of
Polyxena. Some of the striking similarities between this Troilo
episode as told by Boccaccio and that of Achilles as told by
Benoit are as follows:[12] (1) Both men are stricken with love

while in a temple at a yearly service. (2) Both, at first, have aloof attitudes toward the women they see at the service. And (3) both, having returned to their homes, suffer the pangs of love and finally summon faithful friends to act as intermediaries. Although Benoit claims to be following only Dares here, he seems to have used Dictys too.[13]

Boccaccio, supplemented by Benoit and probably by Guido, was the main source of Chaucer's *Troilus and Criseyde*.[14] About a third of the lines in Chaucer's poem are adaptations from the *Filostrato*.[15] Nevertheless, the English work is much longer and much more complex than its Italian model. Chaucer has transformed Boccaccio's characters into fuller, richer beings and has touched the prevailing sadness of the story with his gentle humor.

Two other important English works which stand in the tradition of the medieval Troy story are Robert Henryson's *Testament of Cresseid* and Shakespeare's *Troilus and Cressida*. Henryson's poem is a sequel to Chaucer's; it tells how Cresseid goes from bad to worse and ends her life as a beggar and leper. Shakespeare's play shows the influence of both Chaucer and Henryson; but it was based primarily on William Caxton's *Recuyell of the Historyes of Troye,* an English translation of a French translation of Guido.[16]

The Anti-Homeric Tradition

Dictys and Dares frequently contradict Homer in spite of the fact that he was obviously the ultimate source of much of what they report. They promise to give more accurate accounts than his.

Both writers actually claim, as we know, to have lived at the time of the Trojan War, whereas Homer lived much later. The one, designating himself Dictys (otherwise unknown), states that he is a follower of Idomeneus, the leader of the Cretans; the other calls himself Dares the Phrygian (perhaps to be identified with the priest of Vulcan first mentioned in *Iliad* 5.9), a follower of the Trojan Antenor. Thus, if we can believe our authors (who often disagree with each other), they are primary sources for the events they describe, and Homer, wherever he fails to agree with them, is wrong. The pro-Trojan Dares tends to be more anti-Homeric than Dictys, perhaps because of the belief (false) that Homer had favored the Greeks.

Dictys and Dares were influenced by two criticisms which had been brought against Homer from very early times. First, Homer was criticized for picturing the gods as thieves and adulterers and for showing them doing battle with mortals. Our authors, on the other hand, present the gods as without human foibles and wholly worthy of worship. Furthermore, they use none of the divine machinery typical of epic poetry, and they tend to describe supernatural occurrences in rationalistic terms. Sometimes Dictys openly flouts the traditional account by offering the reader a choice between rational and supernatural explanations.[17]

Secondly, Homer was accused of playing favorites with certain heroes. Why, for instance, does he completely ignore Palamedes and mention Troilus only once? Our anti-Homeric authors emphasize these and other characters slighted by Homer. Dares does this especially, for in his account Palamedes and Troilus play more prominent roles than in Dictys' version. Polyxena is another character never mentioned by Homer: Achilles does not fall in love with her in the *Iliad* as he does in Dictys and Dares.

Homer's Achilles is the embodiment of the heroic ideal according to which the virtues of manly courage and personal honor are prized above long life and ease. The opposite of this ideal is represented by Paris who, being enamored of Helen, sacrifices the good of his country to satisfy his desire. Soon after Homer the heroic ideal began to be debased; and finally, as in the works of our authors, it disappeared altogether. The great

Achilles becomes no better than Paris. In the traditiona¹ account
an heroic Achilles meets his end while fiercely attacking the city
of Troy.[18] In Dictys and Dares an enamored Achilles is ambushed
and killed in the temple of the Thymbraean Apollo, a neutral
zone, where he has come to bargain with the enemy for Polyxena's
hand in marriage.[19]

The middle ages were even more anti-Homeric than later
antiquity. In Western Europe, the knowledge of Greek, and therefore of Homer, died out. Medieval writers, as we have seen, based
their accounts on Dictys and Dares; furthering the anti-Homeric
tendencies they found in these sources, they created the romance
of Troilus and Cressida.[20]

Belief in the truth of Dictys and Dares survived the Revival
of Learning. Not until the beginning of the eighteenth century did
Jacob Perizonius, once for all, prove that our authors were
forgers.[21]

Dictys

All our manuscripts of Dictys are written in medieval Latin.
They can be divided into two groups, each of which has a separate
introduction. The manuscripts of one group are introduced by a
Preface, those of the other group are introduced by a Letter.[22]

The author of the Letter makes three claims: (1) He is the
Latin translator of an original Greek Dictys; (2) he has made a
free, not a literal, translation; and (3) while reproducing the first
five books of the original complete, he has condensed the last
books into one.[23]

For a long time many scholars were unable to believe that a
Greek Dictys had ever existed. Finally, however, in the winter
of 1899-1900 a Greek papyrus fragment closely corresponding
to a portion of our Latin text was found on the back of income
tax returns for the year 206 A.D.[24] Thus our Latin Dictys, which

we know was composed much later than the Greek of the papyrus fragment, was proved to be a translation of a Greek original. Furthermore, the papyrus fragment helps us to prove that this is a free translation, and that its last book is an abridgment.

The following comparison of the same passage (Dictys 4.9) in the Greek papyrus fragment and in the Latin translation clearly illustrates the much greater fullness of the latter.

> πένθος δὲ οὐ μικρὸν τοῖς ἐν Ἰλίῳ ἐγένετο
> Τρωίλου ἀπολομένου· ἦν γὰρ ἔτι νέος καὶ
> γενναῖος καὶ [ὡραῖος].[25]

> Troiani tollunt gemitus et clamore lugubri
> Troili casum miserandum in modum deflent
> recordati aetatem eius admodum immaturam
> qui in primis pueritiae annis cum verecundia
> ac probitate, tum praecipue forma corporis
> amabilis atque acceptus popularibus adolescebat.[26]

Moreover, even before the discovery of the papyrus fragment, it was quite certain that the Latin Dictys could not be a literal translation of a Greek original, for its style is heavily indebted to earlier Latin literature. The translator has imitated Plautus, Terence, Cicero, Livy, Caesar, Cornelius Nepos, Vergil, and especially Sallust.[27] The influence of Sallust has been detected in more than 350 places.[28] For instance, in the passage quoted above, *acceptus popularibus,* for which there is no equivalent in the Greek, is probably derived from the Sallustian *tam acceptum popularibus.*[29]

In spite of the fact that the Latin Dictys is a free translation, it seems for the most part to represent faithfully the essential matter of the original. The freedom of the translator consisted in embellishing the bare bones of the Greek, often by drawing appropriate phrases from earlier Latin authors. Even so, his own work is exceptionally dry and straightforward.

The fullness of the translation in the above passage from Book 4 of the Latin Dictys also tends to confirm the claim of the author of the Letter to have translated the first five books without abridgment, for the rest of the Latin text in Books 1 through 5 seems equally as full as this passage.

On the other hand, in comparison with Books 1 through 5, Book 6, with which the Latin Dictys ends, seems very compressed; it attempts to summarize the whole story of the return of the Greeks after the Trojan War. Furthermore, the Byzantine writer Malalas, whose work was derived from the Greek Dictys, gives a much longer and more detailed account of the returns than that of the Latin Dictys.[30]

We also know, from two other Byzantine sources, that the Greek Dictys contained nine books.[31] Thus we can conclude that the first five books of our Latin text are a fairly faithful reproduction of the first five books of the original Greek, but that Book 6 of our text is a condensation of the last four books of the Greek.

Since the author of the Letter has correctly described the composition of our Latin Dictys, we have every reason to believe that he was the one who composed it. The heading of the Letter gives his name as Lucius Septimius; unfortunately, this is all we know about him.

We can date the composition of the Letter and the Latin Dictys to the fourth century A.D. First, considerations of language and style point to this time. Secondly, the word *consularis* which is used in the Letter, with reference to Rutilius Rufus, to mean "governor of a province" did not acquire this sense until the reign of Constantine (323-337 A.D.).[32]

The Quintus Aradius Rufinus to whom the Letter is addressed is probably to be identified with an Aradius Rufinus who was a commander of the east in 363 A.D. There is, however, another possible identification, for we also know of a Quintus Aradius Rufinus who was a prefect of Rome in the fourth century A.D., but in the early years before Constantine's reign.[33]

Both the Letter and the Preface (which introduces the other group of Latin manuscripts) describe how the Greek Dictys was originally composed and how it was eventually discovered. They do not, however, give exactly the same account. For instance, in the Preface an earthquake lays open Dictys' tomb, and shepherds take the manuscript to Eupraxides; whereas in the Letter the tomb collapses from old age, and the shepherds take the manuscript to Praxis.[34]

N. E. Griffin has given the following explanation for these two introductions: Our Latin Preface represents the original Greek Preface written by the author of the Greek Dictys; its genuineness is indicated by the fact that it gives "more specific and circumstantial" readings, such as the name Eupraxides instead of Praxis. The author of the Letter is, as he says, the Latin translator of the Greek Dictys; the Greek Preface, which he must have read somewhere, was missing from the Greek manuscript he used to make his Latin translation, and this is why he thought it necessary to reproduce the information of the Preface in his Letter, and why his Letter disagrees with the Preface to such an extent.[35]

Accordingly, probably after our Latin Dictys, along with its introductory Letter, had been composed, another translator must have turned the Greek Preface into Latin. Perhaps he had read the Letter but preferred the Preface as the original and therefore truer introduction.

If, as seems likely, the author of the original Dictys wrote the Preface as an introduction to his work (thus playing the roles of two men who lived a thousand years apart), we can date the original to after 66 A.D.—"the thirteenth year of Nero's reign"—when the Preface claims that it was discovered. Furthermore, we know, on the basis of palaeographical evidence, that the Greek

papyrus fragment was written before 250 A.D.[36] Thus the original
Dictys must have been composed between 66 A.D. and 250 A.D.
Griffin argues for a date soon after Nero's reign; he points out
that "occasional variations in the fragment from what we must
suppose to have been the original Dictys' memoirs" (that is, where
the fragment omits details contained in both the Latin Dictys and
Malalas) tend to support this view.[37]

The name "Dictys" is probably derived from "Dicte," the
name of the famous mountain on Crete; "Dictaean" is a synonym
for "Cretan." Our author throughout his work shows a bias toward
the Cretans: for instance, Idomeneus, the leader of the Cretans,
is the one to whom Ulysses tells his adventures. Accordingly, we
can surmise that our author was probably a Cretan. To judge from
his work, he seems to have had the typical Cretan character as
described in the following New Testament text of the first century
A.D.: "One of themselves, even a prophet of their own, said, The
Cretians are always liars, evil beasts, slow bellies. This witness
is true."[38]

The title of our author's work, in Latin, is *Ephemeris Belli
Troiani* (*A Journal of the Trojan War*). The word *ephemeris* is
borrowed from the Greek, and must have stood in the Greek
original. It means "diary" or "journal" and is often used in the
sense of a military record. Thus the Greek writer Plutarch refers
to Caesar's *Commentarii* as *Ephemerides*.[39] Caesar's *Gallic War*
is a military record written in a simple prose style by a man who
took part in the events which he describes; and this is exactly
what Dictys' *Trojan War* purports to be.

Dares

Dares is known to us only in a medieval Latin version. This
Latin Dares is introduced by a Letter whose author claims that he
is the Latin translator of an original Greek Dares and that he has

made a word-for-word translation. Since no papyrus fragment of
a Greek original has as yet been found, we must test these claims
in other ways.

Schissel von Fleschenberg has given two main reasons for
believing that a Greek text of Dares once existed.[40] First, our
Latin text, for the description of heroes and heroines in Sections
12 and 13, depends on the same source as the Byzantine writer
Malalas, who knew no Latin. Secondly, the influence of a Greek
original can be detected in the wording of the Latin translation.
There are, moreover, references to Dares which go as far back
as Ptolemy Chennos in the first century A.D., probably soon after
the Greek text of Dares was composed.[41]

Thus we are able to grant that the author of the Letter is,
as he says, the translator of an original Greek work. His other
claim, however, to have made a simple word-for-word translation,
cannot be entirely true. Schissel von Fleschenberg has described
our Latin Dares as a compilation consisting of the following
parts:[42] (1) a history of events before the Trojan War (Sections
1-10) which the translator-compiler has taken from Latin sources
and prefixed to his work; (2) the remains, in Latin translation, of
an original Greek Preface to be found in the Letter and in Sections 12 (beginning) and 44; and (3) the translation of the Greek
Dares (Sections 11-43).

Sections 1 through 10 describe events which happened before the Trojan War, such as the adventure of the Argonauts. This
in itself is enough to make us suspect that they never belonged to
the original Dares. The case against them is conclusively proved
by the fact that they are derived from Latin, and not from Greek,
sources. They betray their Latin origin in mistakes no Greek
would make: for instance, Pelias is called the king of the Peloponnese! Sections 5 through 10 are based on the work of the Latin
author Dracontius.[43]

These additions by the Latin translator-compiler enable us
to date the composition of the Latin Dares to the early sixth cen-

tury A.D. Dracontius, at the beginning of this century, supplies the *terminus post quem*. The *terminus ante quem* is set by a Latin work, composed about fifty years after Dracontius, which is based on Sections 1 through 3 of our text.[44]

The heading of the Letter—"Cornelius Nepos sends greetings to Sallustius Crispus"—may have been added in later medieval times. If not, the translator-compiler is pretending to have done his work in the late first century B.C., when Nepos and Sallust lived. It seems not improbable that he adopted this idea from an original Greek Preface, which told how the Roman scholar Nepos had discovered Dares' work in Athens. Thus we have a Letter and a Preface for Dares whose relationship is very similar to that of the Letter and the Preface which introduce Dictys.

The Dares-Letter is, in fact, more like a preface than a letter.[45] It seems to be addressed to the public in general and not to any particular person, for the author speaks of his "readers," whom he exhorts to judge the worth of Dares' work. Nor does he end, as is customary in letters, with any *vale*; instead, we are simply told to start reading Dares.

The Letter shows signs that it is dependent on an original Greek Preface by the similarity of its contents to that of two other places in our text which speak of Dares in the third person and give information of a prefatory character. (An eyewitness reporter, like Dictys when referring to himself, speaks in the first person.) These places are Sections 12 (beginning) and 44, and form, respectively, an introduction and a conclusion to the main work in Sections 12 through 43. The first place tells how Dares the Phrygian, who wrote this history, did military service until the capture of Troy, and how he saw the major personages during times of truce or when fighting. The second tells how Dares the Phrygian stayed on at Troy as a faithful follower of Antenor, and how the *Acta Diurna* that Dares wrote gives the number of casualties on both sides.

The connection with Antenor, which is comparable to Dictys'

connection with Idomeneus, explains how Dares was able to survive the War and so to write his history. Antenor had helped the Greeks to bring the War to an end, and they, being grateful, had left him and his party unharmed.

The Latin words *acta diurna* are the translation of the Greek *ephemeris,* and thus *Ephemeris (Journal)* must have stood in Dares' original title, just as in Dictys'. The Letter lends force to this conclusion with its assertion that "the history was written, as the title indicates, in Dares' own hand," for the word *ephemeris,* like our word "diary," connotes the penman.[46]

The present title, in Latin, is *De Excidio Troiae Historia (The Fall of Troy, A History)*. It was probably added later by someone who was influenced by the first sentence of the Letter which speaks of "the history which Dares the Phrygian wrote about the Greeks and the Trojans."[47]

Dares' work, as contained in Sections 11 through 43, is much shorter than that of Dictys, Books 1 through 5, which cover practically the same material. The question, therefore, arises whether our Latin translation has abridged the original Greek. The answer to this question, in the absence of any papyrus fragment, cannot be given with certainty. Schissel von Fleschenberg argues, on the basis of the artistic unity of the Latin translation, that our text offers, with some exceptions,[48] a reliable reproduction of the original. He divides Dares' work into an introduction (Sections 11-18) and the ephemeris proper (Sections 19-43). The introduction, he feels, with its character sketches of the chief personages involved, its foretelling of the War's result by means of an oracle, and its description of the short war with Teuthras as a sort of prelude to the main event, shows parallels with the Greek romances, such as the *Ephesian Tale* by Xenophon of Ephesus; and the ephemeris proper reveals its orderly composition in the chronological references which begin almost all of its sections.

We know no more about Dares' original author than we do

about Dictys'. He was, however, to judge from the remarks about Athens and the Athenians in the Letter and from the pro-Athenian bias to be found in his work, probably an Athenian.[49] He makes the Athenian leaders play greater parts than they do in Homer; and his Palamedes—who never appears in Homer and whom the Athenians favored above Ulysses—takes over the role of the seldom mentioned Ulysses and, for a while, replaces Agamemnon as commander-in-chief of the Greeks.

The Translation

Dictys' Latin prose is simple and fairly good. Dares', on the other hand, is very bad; it is, as Gilbert Highet says, "of extreme simplicity, verging on stupidity."[50] My English translations are simple, too, but not so simple, I hope, as to verge on stupidity. I have tried to translate accurately, but not word for word, or even sentence for sentence. Sentences in my translation do not always correspond exactly, in structure or extent, with those of the Latin text. Sometimes I have used a proper name instead of a pronoun, or even instead of an alternate proper name, such as "Neoptolemus" for "Pyrrhus." Thus I have striven for clarity and readability as well as for accuracy.

The Latin texts which I have used for my translations are Werner Eisenhut's 1958 edition of Dictys[51] and Ferdinand Meister's 1873 edition of Dares.[52]

There is, to my knowledge, no previous complete translation of Dictys in English. There is, however, a translation of the first three books in an unpublished thesis by William Huie Hess.[53]

The only previous English translations of Dares which I have been able to find are both based on inferior Latin texts. The first of these was made by Thomas Paynell in 1553.[54] The second was made by Margaret Schlauch in 1928; she used as her text the Delphin edition of 1825.[55]

A

JOURNAL

OF THE

TROJAN WAR

by

Dictys of Crete

TRANSLATED FROM GREEK INTO LATIN

BY

LUCIUS SEPTIMIUS

Letter[1]

Lucius Septimius sends greetings to Quintus Aradius Rufinus.

Dictys of Crete originally wrote his *Journal of the Trojan War* in the Phoenician alphabet, which Cadmus and Agenor[2] had spread throughout Greece. Dictys had served in the War with Idomeneus.

After many centuries the tomb of Dictys at Cnossos (formerly the seat of the Cretan king) collapsed with age.[3] Then shepherds, wandering near the ruins, stumbled upon a little box skillfully enclosed in tin. Thinking it was treasure, they soon broke it open, but brought to light, instead of gold or some other kind of wealth, books written on linden tablets. Their hopes thus frustrated, they took their find to Praxis,[4] the owner of that place. Praxis had the books transliterated into the Attic alphabet (the language was Greek)[5] and presented them to the Roman Emperor Nero.[6] Nero rewarded him richly.

When these little books had by chance come into my hands, I, as a student of true history, was seized with the desire of making a free translation into Latin; I felt I had no special talent but wanted only to occupy my leisure time. I have preserved without abridgment the first five volumes which deal with the happenings of the War, but have reduced into one volume the others[7] which are concerned with the Return of the Greeks. Thus, my Rufinus, I have sent them to you. Favor my work as it deserves, and in reading Dictys. . . .

Preface

Dictys, a native of Crete from the city of Cnossos and a contemporary of the Atridae,[1] knew the Phoenician language and alphabet, which Cadmus brought to Achaea.[2] He accompanied the leaders Idomeneus and Meriones with the army that went against Troy. (Idomeneus and Meriones were the sons of Deucalion and Molus respectively.) They chose him to write down a history of this campaign. Accordingly, writing on linden tablets and using the Phoenician alphabet, he composed nine volumes[3] about the whole war.

When he returned to Crete, he was an old man. On his deathbed he gave instructions that his books be buried with him. In accordance with his wishes they put the linden tablets in a little tin box and hid it in his tomb.

Time passed. In the thirteenth year of Nero's reign an earthquake struck at Cnossos and, in the course of its devastation, laid open the tomb of Dictys in such a way that people, as they passed, could see the little box. And so shepherds who had seen it as they passed stole it from the tomb, thinking it was treasure. But when they opened it and found the linden tablets inscribed with characters unknown to them, they took this find to their master. Their master, whose name was Eupraxides, recognized the characters, and presented the books to Rutilius Rufus, who was at that time governor of the island. Since Rufus, when the books had been presented to him, thought they contained certain mysteries, he, along with Eupraxides himself, carried them to Nero.[4]

Nero, having received the tablets and having noticed that they were written in the Phoenician alphabet, ordered his Phoenician philologists to come and decipher whatever was written. When this had been done, since he realized that these were the records of an ancient man who had been at Troy, he had them translated into Greek; thus a more accurate text of the Trojan War was made known to all. Then he bestowed gifts and Roman citizenship upon Eupraxides, and sent him home.

The Greek Library, according to Nero's command, acquired this history that Dictys had written, the contents of which the following text sets forth in order.

Book One

|1| All the kings who were great-grandsons of Minos, the son of Jupiter, and who ruled over Greece, came to Crete to divide the wealth of Atreus. Atreus, the son of Minos,[1] when making his last will and testament, had left all his gold and silver, and even his herds, to them; for they were his grandsons, the sons of his daughters. Everything was to be equally divided among them, excepting only the rule of his cities and lands. This he bequeathed to Idomeneus, the son of Deucalion, and Meriones, the son of Molus.

Among those who came to Crete were Palamedes and Oeax, the sons of Clymene and Nauplius.

Also Menelaus and his older brother Agamemnon, the sons of Aerope and Plisthenes,[2] came to get their share. (They had a sister, Anaxibia, who at that time was married to Nestor.) People often thought that their father was Atreus, because when their real father, Plisthenes, died young without having made a name for himself, Atreus, pitying their plight, had taken them in and brought them up like princes.

In the division of Atreus' property everyone, as befitted his rank, acquired a handsome inheritance.

|2| All the descendants of Europa (she was worshiped on Crete with the most elaborate ritual), on learning that the heirs of Atreus had landed, hastened to give them a friendly welcome. Escorting them to the temple, they entertained them lavishly with elegant banquets, offering, in accordance with their ancient cus-

toms, many sacrificial victims. Thus, day after day, the kings of Greece delighted in this entertainment. They were, however, even more impressed by the temple of Europa itself, so magnificent was the beauty of this structure, so rich its embellishments. Examining all its marvelous features, they called to mind how Europa's father, Phoenix, and the noble matrons, had brought across from Sidon this thing and that.

|3| During the same time the home of Menelaus at Sparta welcomed Alexander the Phrygian,[3] the son of Priam, who had come with Aeneas and other of his relatives. Alexander, taking advantage of Menelaus' absence, committed a very foul crime. Falling desperately in love with Helen, the most beautiful woman in Greece, he carried her off, along with much wealth, and also Aethra and Clymene, who, being Menelaus' relatives, attended on Helen.

A report of this crime came to Crete;[4] but rumor, as commonly happens, spread over the island, making what Alexander had done seem worse than it was. People were even saying that King Menelaus' home had been taken by storm and that his kingdom was conquered.

|4| On learning this news, Menelaus was deeply upset by the abduction of his wife, but he was even more disturbed by the fact that the relatives we mentioned above had wronged him.[5]

Palamedes noticed that the king, being distraught with wrath and righteous indignation, had lost all power of reason. Accordingly, he rigged the ships and brought them to shore equipped with all their gear. Loading as much of Menelaus' inheritance as time under the circumstances allowed, and briefly but appropriately offering his sympathy, he made the king go aboard. And thus, the winds blowing as they desired, they came to Sparta within a few days.

Agamemnon, Nestor, and all the rulers of Greece who were descendants of Pelops,[6] having heard the news, had already gathered together at Sparta. On learning of Menelaus' arrival, they all assembled together. First, though the barbarity of the deed demanded immediate vengeance, they decided to send envoys to Troy. Palamedes, Ulysses, and Menelaus were chosen to go, and instructed to complain of the crime and demand the return of Helen and the things that had been carried off.[7]

|5| These, on coming to Troy within a few days, did not find Alexander at home; for when he had sailed from Sparta, hastily and taking no thought of the weather, the winds had forced him to Cyprus. After obtaining some ships, he had then gone on to Phoenicia, where the king of the Sidonians received him kindly. But he treacherously slaughtered the king at night and, venting again that criminal lust he had shown at Sparta, pillaged the palace. He shamelessly ordered his men to seize everything the purpose of which was to show the royal magnificence, and carry it off to the ships. The Sidonians, however, who escaped the general destruction, raised a huge tumult, bewailing the fate of their ruler. All of their people rushed to the palace, and then, arming themselves as best they were able, rushed to the ships; for Alexander had already seized whatever he wanted and now was hastening to sail. A raging battle arose, and very many men fell on both sides. While the Sidonians fought fiercely in the cause of their murdered king, the Trojans strove with all their might to keep the booty they had gained. Two of their ships were fired; but finally, after a terrible struggle, they freed the others. And thus, having broken the strength of their foe, they escaped.

|6| Meanwhile, at Troy, one of the envoys, Palamedes (he was known as a skillful adviser and diplomat), prevailed upon Priam to let him speak at a meeting of the council. First, he made his complaint, describing the criminal way Alexander had broken the ties of mutual friendship. Next, he warned of the horrible conflict that Greece and Troy might have because of this act, citing, among other examples, the feud between Ilus and Pelops,[8] who

for similar reasons had come to the point of committing their countries to war. And then, comparing the hazards of war with the blessings of peace, he said that he knew that most of the Trojans hated this barbarous crime; all would abandon those who were guilty, and the guilty would have to pay for their impious acts.

Palamedes wanted to finish his speech, but Priam interrupted and said: "I beseech you, Palamedes, to go more slowly. It seems unfair to attack a man who is absent, who, if he were present, might refute the criminal charges you are bringing against him." Thus Priam ordered Palamedes to defer his complaint until Alexander arrived. He had noticed that everyone who was present in the council was being moved by Palamedes' speech; though they were silent, nevertheless they showed by their faces that they were condemning the things Alexander had done. Palamedes was making his points with marvelous eloquence, and there was a certain indescribable force in the moving tone of his speech.

Then the council broke up for that day. The envoys went home with Antenor, happy to be his guests. He was a gracious host and a man who, more than anyone else, loved the good and the true.

|7| Several days having passed, Alexander came with the companions we mentioned above, and also with Helen. Upon his arrival, all of the people showed their disgust at what he had done: some cursed the evil precedent he had set; others bewailed the injustice Menelaus had suffered. And finally, disgusted and angry, they raised a revolt.

Priam, alarmed by this turn of events, called together his sons and asked what course they advised. They answered unanimously that, no matter what happened, Helen should not be returned. They saw, no doubt, that if this were done, they would lose all the great wealth with which she had come. Furthermore, they had fallen in love with the beautiful women who had come with Helen and had already set their hearts on marrying this or that one. Being barbarians in language and morals, and impatient of weighing their actions or asking advice, they were driven astray by greed for booty and lust.

|8| Leaving his sons, Priam called together the elders. After reporting what his sons had decided, he asked each member to give his advice. This was the custom. But before anyone could state his opinion, the princes suddenly broke into the council and—never before had this happened—threatened all of the members: they had better not find anyone opposing their will.

Meanwhile all of the people were cursing and crying out against the crime Alexander had committed and against many other similar acts. This caused Alexander, who was reckless because of his lust, to surround himself with his brothers in arms and make an attack on the crowd; for he feared that something might happen to him at the hands of the people. Many were killed, but finally the slaughter was stopped by those who had been in the council, the nobles led by Antenor. Thus the people returned to their homes, their numbers not undiminished, frustrated as to their goals and held in contempt.

|9| On the following day King Priam, at the insistence of Hecuba, went to Helen. Greeting her kindly, he urged her to feel well disposed and asked who she was and what was her family.

She answered that she was Alexander's relative and more closely akin to Priam and Hecuba than to the sons of Plisthenes. She went through the whole list of her ancestors. Danaus and Agenor were the progenitors, respectively, of Priam's line and of hers.[9] The daughter of Danaus was Hesione,[10] who had given birth to Electra by Atlas; Electra had given birth to Dardanus by Jupiter; and from Dardanus were descended Tros and, in order of succession, the other kings of Troy. As for Agenor, he had begotten Taygete; and she had given birth to Lacedaemon by Jupiter; Lacedaemon had begotten Amyclas, and he had begotten Argalus, the father of Oebalus; it was well known that Oebalus was the father of Tyndareus, and he, it seemed, was her father. She also recited the relation of her mother's family with Hecuba, for the son of Agenor, Phoenix, was the ancestor both of Leda and of Hecuba's father, Dymas.

After revealing her whole genealogy, she burst into tears and begged him not to return her. Now that the Trojans had made her welcome, and she had put her trust in them, they must not prove faithless. Everything Alexander had taken from Menelaus' home belonged to her; nothing else had been taken.

It was by no means clear why she preferred to look after her interests in this way. Was it because of her immodest love for Alexander, or because of her fear of the punishment her husband would exact for desertion?

|10| When Hecuba was informed of Helen's attitude and of the relation between their families, she embraced her and did everything she could to prevent her being returned. But by this time Priam and most of the princes were saying that they could no longer put off the envoys or resist the will of the people. (Deiphobus was the only one who sided with Hecuba, for his judgment, like Alexander's, had been corrupted by his lust for Helen.) Hecuba, however, persisted to intercede in Helen's behalf and accosted Priam and all of her sons who were present. They found it impossible to pull her from Helen's embrace and, therefore, finally decided to do as she wished. Thus by her influence as mother and wife she compromised the good of her country.

On the next day Menelaus, accompanied by the other envoys, came into the assembly. He demanded the return of his wife and the things Alexander had taken.

Then Priam, standing in the midst of the princes and calling for silence, said that Helen (who had come into public view for this purpose) should have the right to decide. When he asked her, "Do you want to go home?" her answer, so they reported, was "No." She had not sailed, she said, unwillingly, for her marriage to Menelaus did not suit her. And so the princes left the assembly, exulting, with Helen.

|11| When they had gone, Ulysses, though he knew that nothing he said would make any difference, argued for argument's sake. He reviewed everything Alexander had done and swore that the Greeks would soon be avenging these crimes. Next, Menelaus, full of wrath and scowling blackly, broke up the meeting with threats of destruction.

When Priam's sons were told what had happened, they secretly swore to kidnap the envoys. They believed, quite rightly, that the envoys, having failed to accomplish their mission, would return to Greece and demand a full-scale war against Troy. Antenor, however, whose pious character we mentioned above, thwarted this plot. Going to Priam, he complained about the conspiracy: Priam's sons were not plotting against the envoys but against himself, and this he would not endure. Soon afterwards he informed the envoys. Thus every precaution was taken; he gave them a guard and, at the first opportunity, sent them home unharmed.

|12| While this was happening at Troy, news of the abduction spread throughout Greece. All the descendants of Pelops foregathered and bound themselves with mutual oaths. If Helen was not returned along with the things Alexander had taken, they swore to make war against Priam.

The envoys, having returned to Sparta, told about Helen's decision and described the hostile words and deeds of Priam and his sons against them. But they praised Antenor in the highest terms for the good faith he had shown. The members of the Greek council, having heard this report, decided to make preparations for war in their different regions and kingdoms. They chose Argos, which was the realm of Diomedes, as a good place to meet and make plans for the war.

|13| When the time seemed best, Ajax the son of Telamon, who

was known for his bravery no less than his hugeness, was the first to arrive, accompanied by Teucer, his brother. Soon afterwards Idomeneus and Meriones came, who were the closest of friends.

(I followed along with these. As to what happened earlier at Troy, I have tried to make my report as accurate as possible, Ulysses being my source. The account that follows, based as it is on my own observations, will meet, I hope, the highest critical standards.)

Also Nestor came to Argos, accompanied by Antilochus and Thrasymedes, his sons by Anaxibia. Then Peneleus came with his cousins Clonius and Arcesilaus; and these were followed by two other leaders of the Boeotians, Prothoenor and Leitus. Schedius and Epistrophus came from Phocis; Ascalaphus and Ialmenus, from Orchomenus. Then Diores and Meges, the sons of Phyleus, came; then Thoas, the son of Andraemon; Eurypylus, the son of Euaemon, from Ormenion; and then Leonteus.

|14| Next Achilles arrived, the son of Peleus and Thetis. (Thetis, so they say, was the daughter of Chiron.) Achilles was in the first years of his manhood, a noble youth and handsome. So great was his zeal for war that he was already known as the bravest champion alive. Nevertheless, it must be admitted, his character showed a certain ill-advised forcefulness, a certain savage impatience. He was accompanied by Patroclus, his close friend, and Phoenix, his guardian and teacher.

Then there was Tlepolemus, the son of Hercules; and after him, Phidippus and Antiphus, the grandsons of Hercules, wearing beautiful armor. After them came Protesilaus, the son of Iphiclus, with his brother Podarces. And Eumelus of Pherae was there. (Eumelus' father, Admetus, had once prolonged his life by having his wife die for him.)[11] Podalirius and Machaon came from Tricca; they, being sons of Aesculapius, had been summoned to serve as physicians. Then Philoctetes came, the son of

Poeas, carrying the marvelous bow and arrows of Hercules, whom he had formerly served. (As reward for his service, Hercules, when departing to be with the gods, had given these weapons to him.)[12] Then the handsome Nireus came. Menestheus came from Athens; Ajax the son of Oileus, from Locris; Amphilochus, the son of Amphiaraus, and Sthenelus, the son of Capaneus, from Argos, and with them was Euryalus, the son of Mecisteus; Thersander, the son of Polynices, came from Aetolia; and, last of all, Demophoon and Acamas. These were all the descendants of Pelops. They were followed by a great number of others, coming from various regions, some being retainers of kings, and others rulers themselves. It seems quite useless, however, to give a list of their names.

|15| When all had assembled at Argos, Diomedes supplied their needs and made them at home. Agamemnon distributed a great amount of gold he had brought from Mycenae, and thus increased their yearning for war. Then they decided unanimously to seal their alliance as follows:

Calchas the prophet, the son of Thestor, having ordered a hog brought into their midst, cut it in half and set the parts towards east and west. Then he commanded them all to draw their swords and pass through the victim. Thus, smearing their blades with the blood of the hog, and completing the other rites as required, they bound themselves to war against Priam. They swore to fight on until Troy and Priam's whole kingdom was utterly destroyed. After taking this oath and purifying themselves with ablutions, they sacrificed many victims to Mars and Concord, seeking the aid of these gods.

|16| Then they decided to appoint a commander-in-chief. Accordingly, in the temple of the Argive Juno, everyone, having received a ballot, wrote (in Phoenician letters) the name of the man he thought would make the best leader. Agamemnon was chosen and thus, with the hearty approval of each and every one,

he took upon himself the command of the forces. He deserved this position for two reasons: first, he was the brother of the man for whose sake they were fighting; and second, he was considered the wealthiest and most powerful king in Greece. Then they appointed Achilles, Ajax, and Phoenix to be the leaders in charge of the fleet; and gave Palamedes, Diomedes, and Ulysses joint command of the army-in-camp, that is, the routine duties of the day and the watches of the night. Having made these arrangements, the Greeks departed to their different kingdoms to get ready their forces and equipment for war.

Zeal for war inflamed all Greece during the following period. Within two years everything was ready; weapons for defense and offense, and horses and ships. The men had accelerated their work, some acting with natural zest, others to rival the glory their comrades were gaining. They felt, understandably enough, that their most important task was the construction of a great naval force; the many thousands of soldiers, when once they had been gathered from everywhere, must not be delayed for want of a fleet. |17| Thus at the end of two years all the kings had equipped ships varying in number with the wealth and power of their kingdoms,[13] and had sent them on to Aulis in Boeotia; this was the place they had chosen. Agamemnon assembled a fleet of 100 ships from Mycenae, in addition to 60 others from the various cities under his power; he put Agapenor in charge. Nestor equipped a fleet of 90 ships. Menelaus had 60 ships from all Lacedaemon; Menestheus 50 from Athens; Elephenor 40 from Euboea; Ajax, the son of Telamon, 12 from Salamis; Diomedes 80 from Argos; Ascalaphus and Ialmenus 30 from Orchomenus; Ajax, the son of Oileus, 40; Arcesilaus, Prothoenor, Peneleus, Leitus, and Clonius 50 from all of Boeotia; Schedius and Epistrophus 40 from Phocis; Thalpius and Diores, along with Amphimachus and Polyxenus, 40 from Elis and the other cities of this region; Thoas 40 from Aetolia; Meges 40 from Dulichium and the islands of the Echinades; Idomeneus and Meriones 80 from all Crete; Ulysses

12 from Ithaca; Prothous 40 from Magnesia; Tlepolemus 9 from Rhodes and the other islands about; Eumelus 11 from Pherae; Achilles 50 from Pelasgian Argos; Nireus 3 from Syme; Podarces and Protestilaus 40 from Phylaca and the other places they controlled; Podalirius and Machaon 30; Philoctetes 7 from Methona and other cities; Eurypylus 40 from Ormenion; Guneus 22 from Perrhaebia; Leonteus and Polypoetes 40 from their regions; Phidippus and Antiphus 30 from the islands of Cos and Crapathus; Thersander (the son of Polynices, as we mentioned above) 50 from Thebes; Calchas 20 from Acarnania; Mopsus 20 from Colophon; and Epeus 30 from the islands of the Cyclades.

They filled their ships with large amounts of grain and other necessary goods. Agamemnon had of course ordered them to do this, that so huge a military force might not be harassed with lack of supplies.

|18| In addition to this huge armada, there were many horses and war chariots, their number being large, considering the lack of good pasture in Greece. The infantry, however, far outnumbered the cavalry. Also there were the many technical experts who were necessary to maintain and operate the ships.

During this time we were unable, either by bribery or by the influence of Phalis,[14] the king of the Sidonians, to entice the Lycian Sarpedon to follow our alliance. Priam, by offering larger gifts (which afterwards were doubled), had already won his support for the Trojans.

It took five years for all the ships (which, as we have described above, were brought together from the various regions of Greece) to be equipped and readied. When, however, nothing except the soldiers' absence prevented us from sailing, all of our leaders, at the same time, as if at a given signal, came together at Aulis.

|19| While we were hastening to sail, Agamemnon (who, as we have said above, had been unanimously chosen commander-in-chief), having gone some way from the camp, noticed a she-goat

grazing near a grove of Diana and, feeling no awe because of the place, struck it through with his spear. Soon afterwards, either because of heavenly wrath or atmospheric contamination, a plague began to attack us. Day after day it raged with greater and greater violence, destroying many thousands as it passed indiscriminately through herds and army, laying waste everything that stood in its way, there being no abatement, no end to death.

While our leaders were seeking some remedy, a certain woman,[15] divinely inspired, revealed the reason for our affliction: the wrath of Diana; the goddess was exacting punishment from the army for the sacrilege of slaying the she-goat in which she especially delighted, nor would she relent until the perpetrator of this awful crime had made full atonement by sacrificing his oldest daughter. When this solution was brought to the army, all of our leaders approached Agamemnon. Begging and then threatening, they tried to make him offer the remedy quickly, but he obstinately and absolutely refused. And so they reviled him and finally stripped him of his command.

But in order that their huge army, being leaderless, might not become an undisciplined mob, they chose four men to share the command: Palamedes, Diomedes, Ajax the son of Telamon, and Idomeneus. And they divided their forces, according to the number of leaders, into four equal parts.

|20| Meanwhile the plague continued to rage until Ulysses unexpectedly provided the necessary remedy. No one knew of his plan. He pretended to return to his kingdom because of his anger at Agamemnon's refusal, but went instead to Mycenae and took Clytemnestra a letter he had forged in the name of her husband. The gist of this letter was as follows: Achilles refused to sail for Troy until he had married their oldest daughter, Iphigenia, whom they had promised to him; therefore, she should send Iphigenia to Aulis, along with the dowry, as quickly as possible. In addition to bringing this letter, Ulysses said many things to strengthen Cly-

temnestra's belief in its contents. Thus she, desiring both to recover her sister Helen and, even more, to marry her daughter to
so famous a man, gladly entrusted Iphigenia to Ulysses. Within
a few days he returned to the camp and appeared unexpectedly
with the girl in the grove of Diana.

When Agamemnon knew what had happened, he wanted to
flee, either because of his love for his- daughter or because he
wanted no part in so criminal a sacrifice. Nestor, however, learned
of his plans and, in a long speech, by means of that art of persuasion in which he was more pleasing and effective than anyone else
in Greece, prevailed upon him to stay.

|21| Ulysses, Menelaus, and Calchas were put in charge of the
sacrifice; everyone else was kept at a distance. When they had
begun to adorn the girl, suddenly, lo and behold, the day began
to darken. Thunder roared and lightning flashed, earth and sea
were shaken. Finally a whirlwind of dust made the darkness complete. Soon afterwards rain and hail poured down. This ghastly
disturbance which showed no signs of abatement threw Menelaus
and the other officiants into confusion; they were caught between
their fear and perplexity. At first they were frightened by the sudden change in the weather and believed that this was the sign of
some god, but then they were worried that the army might suffer
some harm if they discontinued the sacrifice. While they were
trying to solve their dilemma, they heard a voice from the grove
saying that divinity spurned such an offering; the goddess had
mercy upon the girl, and they must not touch her; as for Agamemnon, after his victory at Troy, his wife would see to his ade-
quate punishment; they must sacrifice what they would see had
been sent in the place of the girl. Then the winds and the lightning
and all the storm's fierceness began to diminish.

|22| While these things were happening, Achilles received a per-
sonal letter from Clytemnestra, and also a great deal of gold; she
commended her daughter and all of her house to him. When he

had read the letter, he realized the scheme of Ulysses and, dropping all other concerns, rushed to the grove, shouting for Menelaus and the other officiants to keep their hands off Iphigenia, or else he would kill them. He found them still in a state of shock; and when the weather had cleared, he freed the girl. But what was the thing, where was the thing that they had been ordered to sacrifice? This was perplexing them all when a marvelously beautiful deer appeared untrembling before the very altar. Accepting this deer as the victim which had been predicted and which was now divinely offered, they seized upon it and soon slew it. With the performance of this sacrifice, the force of the plague subsided, and the sky became bright as in summer. Then Achilles and the three officiants, acting in complete secrecy, entrusted the girl to the king of the Scythians, who was there at this time.[16]

|23| Our leaders were all delighted, for they saw that the force of the plague had abated and that the winds were good for sailing, the sea being calm as in summer. Going to Agamemnon and consoling him over his daughter's death, they made him commander-in-chief again. This greatly pleased the whole army, for all the soldiers loved Agamemnon, thinking that he would look after their interests no less than a father. Agamemnon showed no signs of knowing what had really happened to Iphigenia. Perhaps he knew. Or had he, having pondered the turns of human fortune, steeled himself to adversity? In either case, resuming his office, he invited the leaders to dinner that day.

Several days later, the weather being good for sailing, our leaders set the army in order; and thus we boarded the ships. We had stowed all sorts of costly supplies which the people who lived near Aulis had given us. Grain, wine, and other necessary foods were furnished by Anius and his daughters; the latter were known as Oenotropae (wine-growers) and priestesses of a holy religion.[17] Thus we sailed from Aulis.

Book Two

|1| The winds drove our whole fleet toward Mysia, and at a given signal we quickly guided all of the ships to shore, where, however, there were guards who opposed our men and prevented them from debarking. These guards had been stationed there by Telephus, who was at that time the ruler of Mysia, to protect his country from overseas enemies. They forbade us to come ashore, or even touch land, until they had told their king who we were. When our men paid no heed to these orders and began, one by one, to debark, the guards relented not in the least but used full force to resist and obstruct us. Thereupon all of our leaders agreed that force must be met with force and, snatching up arms and rushing from the ships, angrily slew some of the guards; and put the others to flight, slaughtering any they happened to catch.

|2| The guards who were first to escape the Greeks went and told Telephus about the hostile horde which had attacked their country and which, having slain some of their number, now was holding the shore. And each of the guards, in proportion to his fear, embellished the story with some additional incident.

On learning this news, Telephus, taking the men he had with him and those who were able to be gathered in the emergency, hastened to encounter the Greeks. When the two sides had drawn up their forces, a great battle ensued. They slaughtered each other at close quarters, the deaths of their comrades spurring them on to fight the more fiercely. It was in this battle that Thersander (the son of Polynices, as we mentioned above) attacked Telephus, and fell at his hands. Thersander had killed many of the Mysians, among whom was a doughty fighter, a favorite of Telephus, chosen by him as one of his generals because of his bravery, strength, and natural ability; these successes had gradually caused Thersander to become elated at the prospects of ultimate victory; and thus, daring to do greater deeds, he was killed. Thereupon Diomedes, remembering the friendship their fathers had started,[1] shouldered Thersander's bloody body and carried it off to be cremated and buried according to custom.

|3| Achilles and Ajax the son of Telamon, seeing that the war was resulting in heavy casualties for our side, divided the army between them and, exhorting their troops as the occasion demanded, attacked the enemy more fiercely, their strength apparently renewed. They themselves were in the front of the fighting, now pursuing those who were fleeing, now opposing, like a wall, those who attacked. Thus even then, by being the first or among the first to fight in every encounter, they had won for themselves, both with our men and with the enemy, an illustrious reputation for bravery.

Meanwhile Teuthranius, having noticed that Ajax was winning great glory in battle, hastened to meet him, and there died fighting, felled by Ajax' spear. Teuthranius was the son of Teuthras and Auge; and the half-brother of Telephus, for they had the same mother.[2]

Telephus, being deeply upset by the death of his brother and seeking for vengeance, attacked the enemy line. Having put to flight those who opposed him, he was doggedly pursuing Ulysses in a vineyard nearby when a vine tripped him up. Thereupon Achilles who, from some distance, had seen what had happened, hurled his spear and pierced the king's left thigh. But Telephus rose quickly and, having drawn out the spear, escaped immediate destruction under cover of a group of his men who had come to the rescue.

|4| At the close of this day, both sides were exhausted, for the battle had raged without break, the leaders joined in fierce combat. The presence of Telephus had especially dampened our spirits, tired as we already were from sailing so far; for Telephus was a tall and powerful man whose deeds of valor rivaled those of his divine father, Hercules. Thus with the coming of night, all were glad to stop fighting. The Mysians returned to their homes, our men to the ships. Great was the number of those who were slain in this battle, but greater still was the number of those who were wounded: no one, or at least very few, escaped without injury.

On the next day both sides sent envoys to make a truce for burying the dead. Thus the bodies were collected, cremated, and buried.

|5| Meanwhile Tlepolemus and the brothers Antiphus and Phidippus (who were sons of Thessalus and grandsons of Hercules, as we mentioned above) learned that Telephus was the ruler of Mysia. Relying for protection on the fact of this kinship, they went and told him who they were, and with whom they had sailed. Finally, after a long conversation, they bitterly accused him of the hostile way he had opposed his own people, pointing out that Agamemnon and Menelaus, who had brought together their army, were descendants of Pelops and therefore not unrelated to him.[3] Then they told him about Alexander's crimes against Menelaus' home and about the abduction of Helen. Telephus therefore, they concluded, should want to aid the Greeks because of his relationship with them, and especially in view of Alexander's violation of the laws of guest-friendship; moreover, Telephus' father, Hercules, had also aided the Greeks by those numerous labors the monuments of which existed throughout Greece.

Telephus, though terribly pained by his wound, answered their charges politely. What had happened, he said, was not his fault, but theirs. He had not known that they who had come were closest friends and cherished relatives. They should have sent ahead messengers to announce their arrival, and he would have gone and met them, bidden them welcome, and made them at home; they would have been his guests, and he would have sent them off with gifts when they thought they must go. As for the expedition against Priam, he refused to take part; he was prevented by the closest bonds of kinship, for his wife Astyoche, the mother of his son Eurypylus, was one of Priam's daughters.

Then he quickly commanded that his people be told to stop preparing for war and freely granted our men the right to debark. Tlepolemus and the other envoys were put in the care of Eurypylus; and thus, their mission accomplished, they returned to the ships to tell Agamemnon and the other nobles about the peace and concord with Telephus.

|6| On learning this news, we gladly stopped preparing for war; and, in accordance with the will of the council, Achilles and Ajax went to Telephus. Seeing he was suffering great pain, they tried to console him and urged him to bear up bravely. Telephus, when his pain allowed him to speak, accused the Greeks of not even sending a messenger ahead to announce their arrival. Then he asked how many of our men were descendants of Pelops, and who these descendants were. Having been told, he insisted that these relatives should come and see him. Thereupon our men, having promised to do as he wished, returned and told the others what he desired.

Accordingly, all of the descendants of Pelops, with the exception of Agamemnon and Menelaus, came together and went to Telephus. He was very grateful and very delighted to see them and received them hospitably with many gifts. Moreover, he showed his kindness by sending grain and ample supplies to all our men who were left at the ships. Noticing, however, that Agamemnon and Menelaus were absent, he begged Ulysses to go and summon them. Upon their arrival, he and they exchanged gifts, as royal custom demanded; and they ordered Podalirius and Machaon, the sons of Aesculapius, to come and treat him. These latter hastened to discover a cure and to offer a suitable treatment for the wound.

|7| When we had been delayed from embarking for several days, and the sea, because of the adverse winds, was becoming increasingly rough, we went to Telephus and asked what was the best time for sailing to Troy from Mysia. The beginning of spring, he said; no other time was good. Thereupon, by unanimous agreement, we returned to Boeotia and, having hauled up our ships, dispersed to spend the winter in our different kingdoms.

During this time of leisure, Agamemnon felt free to blame Menelaus for having betrayed Iphigenia,[4] for he believed that he had advised this and was, so to speak, the cause of his grief.

|8| And during this time the Trojans learned of our hostile alliance from the barbarous Scythians, who bartered their goods with the people who lived up and down both sides of the Hellespont. Fear and sorrow prevailed throughout Troy. Everyone who had from the beginning disapproved of Alexander's crime swore that Greece had been wronged and that all of the Trojans, because of the sins of a few, were going straight to destruction. To meet this threat to their country, Alexander and his wicked advisers sent men, carefully chosen from every group, to levy forces in the neighboring regions, and commanded them to return as quickly as possible with their mission accomplished. Thus the sons of Priam sped up preparations in order that, when the army was ready, they might set sail first and carry the entire war to Greece.

|9| Meanwhile Diomedes, having learned what was happening at Troy, quickly went throughout Greece; he met with all of our leaders and told them the plan of the Trojans. We must, he urged, gather supplies and equipment and sail as soon as we could.

Thus we assembled at Argos; but there Agamemnon aroused the wrath of Achilles by refusing to sail. He was still crushed with grief because of the loss of his daughter. Finally, however, Ulysses revived his spirits and sense of purpose by letting him know what had really happened to Iphigenia.

Everyone was present at Argos, and no one neglected his military duty. But Ajax the son of Telamon, along with Achilles and Diomedes, had shown the greatest concern and zeal in preparing for war; and now these saw to the construction of extra ships with which to make beachheads on Trojan territory, building within a few days fifty such vessels complete in all points.

Eight years had passed from the time we first began preparing for war, and now the ninth had begun.

|10| When nothing prevented our sailing, the ships being ready and the sea being calm, we hired Scythians to act as our guides.[5] They had landed at Argos to barter their goods.

At the same time Telephus hastened to sail to Argos to find relief for the wound he had received while fighting our men. Having suffered a long time and found no remedy, he had gone to the oracle of Apollo, and there been told to consult Achilles and the sons of Aesculapius. He reported the oracle to all of our leaders, who were wondering why he had come, and begged them—they were his friends—not to deny the predicted remedy. On hearing his plea, Achilles, Machaon, and Podalirius treated his wound, and thus soon proved the oracle true.

After we had made many sacrifices and besought the gods to aid our endeavors, we went to Aulis, taking the ships mentioned above.

And from there we hastened to sail. Telephus, being grateful because of his cure, offered himself as a guide. Thus we boarded the ships and, finding favorable winds, came to Troy several days later.

|11| Meanwhile the Lycian Sarpedon, the son of Xanthus and Laodamia, in answer to the summons which frequent messengers

had made for Priam, had led a huge army to Troy. Having noticed
from afar that our great armada was landing, he realized the
situation and, alerting his forces, rushed to prevent our debark-
ing. Soon afterwards the sons of Priam learned what was happening and, taking up arms, ran to the aid of Sarpedon. Thus we were
fiercely attacked in every way. At first we could neither debark
without being killed nor arm ourselves, the general confusion
causing our every action to flounder. Finally, however, some,
in spite of the terrible pressure, were able to arm and, banding
together, fiercely counter-attacked. In this battle Protesilaus,
whose ship had been first to land, fell among those who were fighting up front, struck by Aeneas' weapon. Also two sons of Priam
were killed. In fact, no one on either side completely escaped
without injury.

|12| Achilles and Ajax the son of Telamon fought with great
glory, their courage sustaining and increasing the confidence of
our men. They struck fear into the enemy, some of whom, having
dared to oppose them, soon were retreating, and all of whom
finally were taking to flight. Thus we, being free for a time from
enemy attack, were able to draw up our ships and set them safely
in order.

Then we chose Achilles and Ajax the son of Telamon, since
they were the bravest, to guard the ships and the army, stationing
them at the ends of our camp to cover our flanks. When everyone
was settled in place, Telephus departed for home. Our army was
very grateful to him for having led us to Troy.

Soon afterwards Cycnus surprised us with a treacherous
attack. He had heard of our coming, for his kingdom was not
far off from Troy. His attack was made against those of our men
who were preoccupied with the burial of Protesilaus. These,
expecting no trouble, were caught unawares and forced to flee in
utter disorder. But soon the rest of our men, those not entrusted
with the burial, learned what was happening and came to the
rescue. Among these was Achilles who encountered and slew

Cycnus along with countless numbers of others; thus those who had fled were relieved.

|13| But frequent raids by the enemy caused heavy casualties to our side and deeply disturbed our leaders. Therefore, the first thing we decided to do was to attack the cities in the region near Troy with a part of our army and wreak general destruction. We began with the kingdom of Cycnus and plundered the country around it. When, however, we invaded and began to fire the capital, where it was said the sons of Cycnus were being reared, the people, that is, the Neandrienses, offered no resistance and begged us to forbear. Weeping, they prayed on bended knee, by all things human and divine, that their city be spared. They were not, they said, to be blamed for the wicked acts of their evil king; they had been innocent and, after his death, had sided with us. Thus they stirred us to pity and saved their city. We required, however, that they hand over the sons of the king, Cobis and Corianus, along with their sister Glauce. Then we gave the girl to Ajax, in addition to his regular share of the booty, a due reward for his valorous deeds. Soon afterwards the Neandrienses came to the camp and sued for peace; they promised to be our allies and to do whatever we ordered.

When this campaign had been finished, we stormed Cilla but refrained from touching Carene, though it was near. Thus we showed our gratitude for the faithful friendship of the Neandrienses, for they were lords in Carene.

|14| At the same time an oracle of the Pythian god was reported to us. We must, it said, choose Palamedes to offer a sacrifice to the Sminthian Apollo; we must all grant Palamedes this honor. Many of us were happy to obey this oracle, remembering the zeal and love Palamedes had shown throughout the army; but some of the leaders disliked him. Nevertheless, whatever our feelings, we did what was ordered and had Palamedes offer a hundred victims in behalf of all the army. Chryses, Apollo's priest in this region, presided over the offering.

Meanwhile Alexander, having learned what was happening, gathered a force of armed men and came to prevent the sacrifice. But before he could reach the temple, the two Ajaxes killed a great number of his men and put him to flight.

Chryses (who, as we have said above, was the priest of the Sminthian Apollo) feared harm from both armies and pretended to favor those from each side who approached him.

During the sacrifice, Philoctetes, who was standing in the temple near the altar, was suddenly bitten by a serpent. Everyone who saw what had happened raised a shout, and Ulysses rushed forward and slew the serpent. Soon afterwards we sent Philoctetes, with a few other men, to be cured of his poison on Lemnos, for the inhabitants of this island, which was sacred to Vulcan, claimed that their priests were wont to cure cases like his.

|15| During the same time Diomedes and Ulysses devised a plot to kill Palamedes.[6] (It is characteristic of human nature to yield to resentments and envy; one does not easily allow oneself to be surpassed by a better.) Accordingly, these two, pretending to have found gold in a well, persuaded Palamedes—they wanted, they said, to share the treasure with him—to be the one to descend. He suspected nothing; and so, when no one else was nearby, they let him down by means of a rope, and then, picking up stones which were lying around, they quickly stoned him to death. Thus Palamedes, the best of men and the army's favorite, one whose counsel and courage had never failed, died in a way he ill deserved, treacherously slain by the most unworthy men. There were those who suspected Agamemnon of having shared in this plot, for Palamedes was very popular with the soldiers, most of whom wanted him as their king and openly said that he should be made commander-in-chief. After burning the body, a ceremony which was attended, like a public funeral, by all the Greeks, the ashes were placed in a golden urn.

|16| Meanwhile Achilles suspected that the states bordering on Troy were Trojan allies and, so to speak, a Trojan arsenal. Ac-

cordingly, taking some ships, he attacked Lesbos and easily took it by storm. Having slain Phorbas, the king of this island, who had committed many acts of hostility against us, he carried off Diomedea, Phorbas' daughter, along with much booty. Then, as all of his soldiers demanded it, he attacked the wealthy cities of Scyros and Hierapolis with all of his forces; and these he utterly destroyed without any trouble within a few days. Wherever he went, the country was completely pacified and plundered, and everything was thrown into turmoil; anything that might be helpful to Troy was either overturned or destroyed. The other neighboring peoples, having learned what was happening, flocked to him in peace and promised him half of their crops if he, in return, would leave their fields unharmed. Thus he made treaties with these and exchanged pledges of peace.

After completing this campaign, Achilles returned to camp, a glorious victor bringing much booty. At the same time the king of the Scythians, having learned that our men had arrived, came and brought many gifts.

|17| But Achilles was by no means content with what he had already done. Therefore, he attacked the Cilicians and, within a few days, took Lyrnessos by storm. Having slain Eetion, the king of Lyrnessos, he filled his ships with much wealth and carried Astynome off, the daughter of Chryses and, at that time, Eetion's wife.

Then Achilles hastened to storm Pedasos, a city of the Leleges. When Brises, the king of the Leleges, saw the fierceness of the siege, he realized that there was no way the enemy could be resisted or his own people sufficiently defended. Despairing of both flight and safety, he returned to his palace and, while everyone else was busy fighting, hanged himself. Soon afterwards the city was taken; many people were killed, and, Hippodamia, the daughter of Brises, was carried off.

|18| During the same time, Ajax the son of Telamon made a

sweeping attack against the Thracian Chersonese. When Polymestor, the king of this region, learned of Ajax' prowess in war,
he thought it was useless to fight and sought terms of surrender.
First, he handed over Priam's son, Polydorus. (Priam, acting in
complete secrecy, had sent this son, soon after birth, across for
Polymestor to raise.) Second, he gave gold and other such gifts,
enough to satisfy his enemy's demands. Third, he promised a
year's supply of grain for our entire army and filled the merchant
ships Ajax had brought for this purpose. When, finally, he had
denounced, with many curses, his treaty with Priam against us, his
plea for peace was deemed acceptable.

After completing this campaign, Ajax turned toward the
country of the Phrygians. He attacked them and slew their ruler
Teuthras[7] in single combat. Within a few days he had stormed
and fired their city and carried off a great amount of booty, including Tecmessa, the daughter of Teuthras.

|19| Then Achilles and Ajax, coming from different directions,
returned to camp at the same time, as if by plan. Having sacked
many cities and laid waste vast regions, they had won great renown
for themselves. When the heralds had assembled all the soldiers
and leaders, the two returning heroes entered the crowd—not
together, but one at a time—and displayed, for everyone to see,
the results of all their labors and pains. Seeing what they had
brought, we shouted their praises, and crowned them, as they
stood in our midst, with wreaths of olive.

In deciding how best to divide the booty, we followed the
advice of Nestor and Idomeneus, the most judicious of men. First,
from the booty that Achilles had brought, Astynome (the wife of
Eetion and the daughter of Chryses, as we said above) was given,
by unanimous decision, to Agamemnon in view of his kingly
office. As for Achilles, he kept Diomedea and also Hippodamia,
the daughter of Brises. It would have been cruel to separate these
girls, for they were of the same age and from similar backgrounds;

furthermore, they had fallen at Achilles' feet and begged him not
to let them be parted. The rest of Achilles' booty was distributed
among the men according to merit.

Then Ajax had Ulysses and Diomedes bring in the booty he
had won. Agamemnon was given as much gold and silver as his
station demanded. As for Ajax himself, he was allowed to keep
Tecmessa, the daughter of Teuthras, a fitting reward for his valorous deeds. The rest of his things were fairly divided, and the grain
was apportioned throughout the army.

|20| When he had finished dividing the booty, Ajax told about
the treaty he had made with Polymestor, and how Polydorus had
been handed over to him. Thereupon we all agreed that Ulysses
and Diomedes should go to Priam and, in return for surrendering
Polydorus, recover Helen along with the things that had been
carried off. While Ulysses and Diomedes were preparing to set
out, Menelaus—this was his business—also joined in the mission.
Thus these proceeded to Troy, with Polydorus' fate resting in their
hands.[8]

When the Trojans beheld our envoys and saw that they were
men of great renown, they hastened to assemble their elders, that
is, those who were wont to hold council. Priam, however, was
kept at home by his sons.

At the meeting of the council Menelaus said that now he had
come a second time, but for the same reason. He complained
about all the wrongs to himself and his house, and especially bewailed the fact that Helen's absence had made an orphan of his
daughter.[9] A former friend, he said, a former guest, had done him
all these wrongs, and he had ill deserved such treatment.

Seeing the depth of his sorrow, the Trojan leaders wept, and
agreed with all he had said, as if they themselves shared in his
wrongs.

|21| Next, Ulysses stood up in their midst and made a speech of
this sort: "Trojan lords, I believe that you know well enough that

the Greeks are not accustomed to begin anything rashly or without proper consideration. From earliest times they have planned and labored that praise rather than blame should attend whatever they do. Let me, without going into details, review that previous occasion when I had dealings with you. As soon as Alexander had attacked and insulted the Greeks, we did not yield to temptation and hasten to arms. This, to be sure, is the usual way for fired-up feelings to seek relief. Instead, as you remember, our council sent us, along with Menelaus, as envoys to seek the recovery of Helen. But we got nothing from Priam and his princes, nothing but haughty, threatening words and hidden treacheries. Therefore, with the failure of our mission, it was to be expected, I think, that we should take up arms and obtain by force what we had been unable to get by friendly means. Thus we have assembled an army with many excellent and famous leaders. But not even so have we determined on war. Rather, following our usual custom and showing our usual moderation, we have come again to implore you in the same cause. Trojans, the rest is in your hands. We will not think less of you for correcting your previously ill-advised actions. Consider only what is wise, and make a sound decision.

|22| "I beg you, by the immortal gods, to ponder what will happen if you make a wrong decision. The effect will be a disaster which will spread, like a plague, throughout the world. After this, when anyone is entering into an important negotiation, will he not, remembering Alexander's crime, find manifold reasons for being suspicious and fearing deceit? Friend will fear friend. Who will open his house even to his own brother? Who will not fear a guest or relative as if he were an enemy? Finally, if you make a wrong decision—and certainly I hope you will not—you will destroy every basis for agreement and mutual understanding between barbarians and Greeks. Therefore, Trojan leaders, do what is good and right, be truly friendly and just. Send the Greeks home

with everything that was stolen from them. Do not wait until our two kingdoms, in spite of their friendship, actually come to hostilities.

"By Hercules, when I think of your plight, I have pity for you. Though you yourselves are innocent and free from fault, nevertheless you must bow to the lusts of a few; and thus the crime of one man will cause you all to be punished. Surely you must know that the Greeks have attacked the cities nearby that are friendly to you and are planning, day after day, to make new attacks. Our success is shown by Polydorus' capture. We will give Polydorus to Priam unharmed when Helen, at long last, is returned with everything that was stolen. If this does not happen, there must be immediate war, continuous war, until one side is completely victorious. Either all the Greek leaders, any of whom could cause your city's destruction, must die or, as I hope, Troy must be captured and fired, and you must become an example of punished impiety for our descendants. I beg you, therefore, I implore you, have foresight, while matters are still in your hands."

|23| When Ulysses had finished speaking, there was a long silence. Everyone, as often happens, was waiting for someone else to speak, someone better than himself. Finally this silence was broken by Panthus, who said in a loud voice: "Ulysses you are addressing people who are unable to do as they please. We are unable to remedy this situation."

And next Antenor said: "Since we are wise and prudent men, we grant you everything you say; and if we had the power, we would advise accordingly. But, as you see, others with whom personal greed counts more than the common welfare are in control of our state."

Then Antenor ordered the leaders of the foreign forces to be introduced: those who had come because of their treaties with Priam, and those who were hired mercenaries.

When these had been introduced, Ulysses made a second

speech. They were all, he said, the wickedest men. They were no
different from Alexander, who was the worst of criminals, for they
had deserted the good and the true to follow him. Each of them
knew that if they approved of this terrible crime they would be
setting an evil example which, being disseminated especially
through the peoples nearby, would serve as a model for similar
or even more sorrowful acts.

Then each of the elders silently pondered how terrible might
be the results of this horrible crime. Being moved to disgust and
shrinking from setting an evil example, they went on record,
voting in their usual way, that Menelaus had suffered injustice.
Only Antimachus, opposing everyone else, voted in Alexander's
behalf. Thereupon they chose two men to go and tell Priam about
all that had happened. And these reported, along with the other
things they were ordered, also about Polydorus.

|24| When Priam heard this report, he collapsed, utterly dumb-
founded, in the presence of all. Soon, however, he got to his feet;
those who were standing around helped to revive him. He wanted
to go to the council, but the princes made him remain while they
themselves went off.

Shortly before they burst into the council, Antimachus had
been hurling reproaches against the Greeks. They had shown
real effrontery, he said, and the Trojans should detain Menelaus
until Polydorus was returned and treat Menelaus exactly as Polydorus was treated.

Everyone was silent to this suggestion with the exception
of Antenor, who, using all the powers at his command, tried to
prevent the council from such a course. He and Antimachus
argued hotly, and finally their passions led them to blows. Then
all the others who were present proclaimed Antimachus an
unruly, seditious person, and drove him out of the council.

|25| As soon as Priam's sons arrived, Panthus begged Hector
(who was believed to be the best of the princes in counsel as well

as in courage) to return Helen peacefully, now that the envoys
had come to regain her. Alexander, he said, had had time enough
to satisfy whatever love he had had for Helen. The Greek kings,
they should remember, were in their country and had recently
sacked cities which were friendly to Troy. Furthermore, these
Greek successes had caused Polymestor willingly to commit the
horrible crime of giving the Greeks Polydorus. The Trojans should
learn from this example and fear that the neighboring regions
might enter into similar schemes and plot the destruction of Troy.
Such an attack would catch the Trojans completely off guard;
bonds of faith would be broken; treachery would reign everywhere; former pacts would be dashed. Therefore, they in the
council should see things as they really were and delay the envoys
no longer, but give Helen up. This act of good will would bring
about a stronger and closer bond of friendship between the Greeks
and the Trojans.

On hearing this, Hector was saddened and wept, remembering his brother's crime. Nevertheless, he thought that Helen should
by no means be given up, for she was a suppliant at his home; good
faith intervened, and they must keep her. If, however, the envoys
would enumerate the various articles that had been carried off
with Helen, all of these things, he thought, should be returned.
And, to take Helen's place, Cassandra or Polyxena, whichever
seemed best to the envoys, should be given in marriage to Menelaus, along with a handsome dowry.

|26| Menelaus was terribly angered at this and answered as fol-
lows: "By Hercules, I am being treated in an excellent manner if I,
who have been robbed of my wife, am forced to marry again according to the will of my enemies."

Then Aeneas replied: "You will not even be granted this
favor since I and the other relatives and friends who advise
Alexander strongly oppose it. Fortunately there are, and always
will be, those who safeguard the house and kingdom of Priam.

The loss of Polydorus does not leave Priam bereft of children, for he still has many other such sons.

"Do you think that abductions, like that of Helen, should be allowed only to those who hail from Greece? The Greeks of Crete, as you know, successfully abducted Europa from Sidon and Ganymede from our kingdom. Medea is another example. She, as surely you know, was abducted from Colchis and carried off to Iolchus. And finally, not to omit your very first of abductions, Io was stolen from Sidon and taken to Argos.

"Up to this time we have merely been bandying words. Now, however, unless you flee our land within a reasonable time, and take your fleet, soon, very soon, you will be tasting Trojan valor and courage. Troy has more than enough young men who are ready for battle, and every day new allies are coming."

When Aeneas had finished this speech, Ulysses said calmly: "Then, by Hercules, there is no need for you to put off hostilities any longer. Give the signal for war and, as you were the first to commit injustice, be also the first to begin the battle. Only provoke us and we will follow suit."

After this exchange of taunts the envoys left the council and departed from Troy.

As soon as the Trojan people learned how Aeneas had answered the envoys, they raised a huge tumult. Aeneas, they thought, was without a doubt a diplomat of the very worst sort; he was the reason why Priam's kingdom was hated and Priam's whole house was headed for ruin.

|27| The envoys, having returned to camp, told all our leaders what the Trojans had said and done to oppose them. Thereupon we determined to kill Polydorus within view of the wall where all the Trojans could easily see what was done. Delaying no further, we led him into the center and stoned him to death in payment for his brother's impiety, while most of the enemy watched from the walls. Then we sent a herald to tell the Trojans

to come and get the body for burial. Idaeus came and, with the help of some slaves of the king, took Polydorus, mangled and torn by the stones, back to his mother, to Hecuba.

Meanwhile Ajax the son of Telamon, in order to keep the enemy riled, attacked the regions nearby that were friendly to Troy. He captured Pitya and Zelia, notoriously wealthy cities, and, not being content with these, laid waste Gargarum, Arisba, Gergitha, Scepsis, and Larissa with marvelous swiftness. Then, having learned from the inhabitants that there were many herds of all sorts being grazed on Mount Ida, since all of his soldiers demanded it, he quickly attacked the mountain and, after killing the herdsmen, drove a large number of cattle away. Then no one opposed him; everyone fled wherever he went; and so, when the time seemed right, he returned to camp, laden with booty.

|28| At the same time Chryses (who was the priest of the Sminthian Apollo, as we have said above), having learned that his daughter, Astynome, was with Agamemnon, came to the ships, trusting in the power of his awesome religion.[10] He brought with him a statue of the god and certain ornaments of the temple, hoping thereby the more easily to remind the kings of the god, and inspire them with awe. Praying for the release of his daughter, he offered gifts of gold and silver, countless ransom. We must, he implored, honor the presence of the god: Apollo was there, begging us in his behalf. Furthermore, because he had recently officiated at our sacrifice, he had incurred the enmity of Alexander and his brothers, who were daily plotting against him.

On hearing his plea, we all thought that the girl should be returned. Nor should we accept any ransom. We owed this to Chryses, not only because of his personal faithfulness to us but, what mattered more, because of his office as priest of Apollo. Having seen many evidences of Apollo's power and having learned of his popularity in the region nearby, we had made up our minds to serve this god devoutly.

|29| When Agamemnon saw what was happening, he proceeded to take a stand opposite to that of everyone else. Scowling blackly and threatening death, he ordered the priest not to return. Accordingly, the old man departed, terrified and fearing for his life, his mission a failure.

When our assembly broke up, our leaders approached Agamemnon, one at a time, and taunted him with his manifold wickedness. Because of his love for a captive girl, he had treated his men, that is, themselves, with contempt and, what seemed a thing most shameful, had scorned a very powerful god.

When all had reviled him, they went away, thinking how he had shared in the plot by which Diomedes and Ulysses had treacherously slain Palamedes, the army's favorite. Achilles openly, in everyone's presence, abused both Agamemnon and Menelaus.

|30| Chryses, after Agamemnon had sent him away unjustly, returned to his home. And several days later a terrible plague invaded our army. Whether this was due to the wrath of Apollo, as everyone thought, or to some other cause, was uncertain. The disease attacked the cattle first and then, as it gradually gained momentum, spread among the men, a great number of whom suffered unspeakable deaths, their bodies slowly wasting away. Except for our leaders (the kings), none of whom died or was even attacked, the plague knew no bounds, and every day saw more men dying. Accordingly, our leaders, each of whom was afraid for himself, foregathered, and ordered Calchas (we have told about his knowledge of the future) to proclaim the cause of this terrible evil.

Although he admitted that he was able to do as they wished, he said that he was by no means free to speak out, for fear he would incur a most powerful king's displeasure. Thereupon Achilles forced all of our kings to swear that they would not be offended, no matter what Calchas might say.

Thus Calchas, feeling that everyone was favorably disposed, announced that the wrath of Apollo was the cause of the plague. Apollo, he said, was angry because of the unjust way we had treated his priest and was therefore exacting punishment from our army.

When Achilles asked what we must do to bring an end to the plague, the prophet said: "Restore the girl!"

|31| Then Agamemnon, though he foresaw what was going to happen, said nothing but withdrew from the council and commanded everyone in his contingent to prepare for war. Achilles, on noticing this, being stirred to wrath and likewise vexed by the horrible way our men were dying, ordered that the bodies of everyone whom the plague had destroyed be collected and thrown out in the assembly for all to see. This was a sight which quickly moved all our leaders and men to desert Agamemnon and follow Achilles, who thereupon urged them to kill Agamemnon unless he repented. Agamemnon, however, when he heard about this, obstinately held to his first decision and refused to yield in the least. It is uncertain whether his inflexibility was due to his naturally stubborn character or to his love for the captive girl.

|32| The Trojans, looking from their walls, saw the many pyres of our dead burning continuously. They also were informed that those of us who were left were growing weak as the plague proceeded to rage. Accordingly, exhorting each other and taking up arms, they rushed from the gates along with their allies and made an attack. Their forces were arranged in the plain in two divisions: Hector was leading the Trojans, Sarpedon the allies.

When we saw them ready for attack, we armed ourselves and, forming an unbroken line of defense, drew up our forces to meet them. Achilles and Antilochus led our right wing; Ajax the son of Telamon and Diomedes led the left; and the other Ajax and Idomeneus, my leader, led the center.

Then the two armies, drawn up in this way, advanced to

attack. As soon as they had come within striking distance, everyone raised the war cry and joined in the battle. The conflict lasted
some time, and the casualties on both sides were heavy. Hector
and Sarpedon were the outstanding leaders among the barbarians;
Diomedes and Menelaus shone among the Greeks. Finally night
brought an end to the battle and rest to the armies. Then both
sides, withdrawing, cremated and buried their dead.

|33| Now the Greeks were on the point of making Achilles com-
mander-in-chief, for he was the one, so we thought, who seemed
most troubled about our misfortunes. And this caused Agamemnon to fear he might lose his glorious position.

Speaking in the council, he said that he was deeply concerned
for the welfare of the army and that Astynome, without any further delay, should be returned to her father, especially if thus we
would rid ourselves of the plague. He asked only to be given Hippodamia, the bond-maid of Achilles, to take the place of the prize
he was losing.

Although everyone thought his request was mean and dishonorable, nevertheless we were moved to grant it. As for
Achilles, to whom Hippodamia had been given because of his
many marvelous deeds, he showed no signs of his feelings; so
great was the love and concern for our army in the heart of this
excellent youth.

Thus Agamemnon was flouting everyone's wishes, but since
no one openly opposed him, he thought that he had our unanimous approval. Accordingly, he ordered attendants to fetch Hippodamia; and they were prompt to obey.

At the same time we had Diomedes and Ulysses take Astynome, along with a great number of sacrificial victims, across to
the shrine of Apollo. When these had completed the sacrifice, the
force of the plague gradually seemed to abate. People were no
longer becoming ill, and those who were already afflicted seemed
to improve, as if their prayers had been divinely answered. Thus

within a short time our entire army regained its usual strength and vigor.

During this period we also sent Philoctetes' share of the booty across to Lemnos, where he was. This was the booty which Ajax and Achilles had won and which we had divided up equally. |34| Achilles, having (as we have described) been treated unjustly, stayed away from our councils. He hated Agamemnon especially; and now his love for the rest of the Greeks was also dead, since they had been silent when he had been robbed of Hippodamia, the reward which his many victories and many brave deeds had earned him. He refused to see any of the leaders who came to visit. Nor would he forgive any of his friends for having deserted him when they might have defended him against Agamemnon's outrageous action. He preferred to stay in his hut with only Patroclus, his closest friend, and Phoenix, his wise teacher, and Automedon, his charioteer.

|35| Meanwhile, at Troy, the allies and mercenaries who had come to help the Trojans began to mutiny. They were probably motivated either by boredom from spending a long time there to no purpose or by longing for those they had left behind in their homelands. Hector, noticing this, felt forced to call his troops to arms; they must be ready to follow whenever he signaled. Then, having been informed that the time looked favorable and that his men were in arms, he ordered them all to go forth, he himself taking command and leading the way.

This seems a good place to list the kings of the allied forces (those who were bound to the Trojans by treaties) and also of the mercenary forces (those who, coming from various regions, were serving Priam's sons for pay).[11] The first to rush from the gates was Pandarus, the son of Lycaon, from Lycia; then Hippothous and Pylaeus, the sons of Lethus,[12] from Pelasgian Larissa; then Acamas and Pirus[13] from Thrace; then Euphemus, the son of Troezenus, who led the Ciconians; Pylaemenes, the boasting

Paphlagonian, whose father was Melius; Odius and Epistrophus, the sons of Minuus, who led the Alizonians; Sarpedon, the son of Xanthus, who led the Lycians, from Solymum; Nastes and Amphimachus, the sons of Nomion, from Caria; Antiphus and Mesthles, the sons of Talaemenes, from Maeonia; Glaucus, the son of Hippolochus, from Lycia, whom Sarpedon had summoned to share the command because he surpassed all other Lycians in counsel and arms; Phorcys and Ascanius from Phrygia; Chromius and Ennomus, who were Mygdonians, from Mysia; Pyraechmes, the son of Axius, from Paeonia; Amphius and Adrastus, the sons of Merops, from Adrestia; Asius, the son of Hyrtacus, from Sestos; and then the other Asius, the son of Dymas and the brother of Hecuba, from Phrygia. Many men followed each of the leaders we have listed; their different customs and different languages caused them to fight in disorder and turmoil.

|36| When our men saw what was happening, we proceeded onto the plain and drew up our forces in battle array. Menestheus, the Athenian, who was in charge of our deployment, set us in order according to our different clans and regions. Only Achilles and his Myrmidons stayed behind. Achilles continued to be angry with Agamemnon for unjustly depriving him of Hippodamia; also the fact that Agamemnon had not invited him to dinner along with the other leaders seemed insulting to him.[14] When our army had been drawn up, we were facing the full force of the enemy for the first time. But neither side dared to begin; both held their ground for a while and then retreated at signals given as if by common consent.

|37| Having returned to the ships, we put down our arms and prepared to enjoy our dinners as usual. We were relaxing, fearing no trouble, when Achilles tried to catch us off guard. There were, however, guards who got wind of his plans and told Ulysses. And Ulysses, running around to all of the leaders, exhorted and warned them, shouting that Achilles was going to attack. They must, he

said, be ready; they must be armed. A great commotion arose, with everyone rushing to arms and striving to save himself. Thus Achilles' plot was disclosed, and he, being foiled, returned to his hut, despairing of any success against our alerted army.

Then our leaders, fearing that this sudden commotion might cause the Trojans to make a new attack, increased the number of the advanced guard. The two Ajaxes, Diomedes, and Ulysses were sent forth. They took up positions where they thought—quite rightly, as it happened—that the enemy would be most likely to come.

Hector, desiring to learn the reason for the uproar in the camp of the Greeks,[15] had persuaded Dolon, the son of Eumedes, with promises of a huge reward, to go and spy. While Dolon, trying to fulfill his mission, was eagerly gathering information, he fell into Diomedes' hands. Diomedes and also Ulysses, who were guarding the area near the ships, made him tell whatever he knew. Then they killed him.

|38| Several days passed without any outbreak of hostilities. Then Greeks and Trojans prepared to lead their armies onto the plain between Troy and the ships. When everything seemed ready for battle, both sides, in full force, cautiously advanced. At given signals the front lines clashed in dense formation. The Greeks fought in good battle order, everyone following the commands of the leader in charge of his division. The barbarians, however, rushed on without any order or discipline. Nevertheless, many on both sides fell in this battle. There was no retreating; everyone attacked and strove to rival the valor of the heroes fighting around him. Among the barbarian leaders who were seriously wounded and forced to withdraw from the battle were Aeneas, Sarpedon, Glaucus, Helenus, Euphorbus, and Polydamas. Among those on our side who were similarly afflicted were Ulysses, Meriones, and Eumelus.

|39| Then Menelaus happened to catch sight of Alexander and

rushed, with all his might, to meet him. Alexander, however, not daring to stay where he was, soon took to flight and escaped. But Hector, having noticed this from a distance, ran forward, along with Deiphobus, and caused Alexander to halt. They reproached him bitterly and finally persuaded him to go out between the battle lines and, when everyone else had grown quiet, challenge Menelaus to single combat.

Thus these brought Alexander back into battle; and he (apparently this was the way to make a challenge) went out in front of the Trojan line. Menelaus, noticing this from a distance, felt that at long last he was being given an opportunity to attack the man he most hated. Right here and now, he thought, Alexander is going to pay with his life for all his crimes. And so he rushed against him again. Signals were given, and everybody on both sides drew back as they saw these two rushing head-on, armed and eager to fight.

|40| Soon the two fighters, taking full strides, had advanced to where they could use their spears. Alexander, hoping to get the start and wound Menelaus, was the first to make a cast. His spear, however, struck against Menelaus' shield, and thus was deflected. Then Menelaus, throwing with all his might, met, alas, with the same result—his spear stuck in the earth; Alexander had been on his guard and dodged the blow. But soon they were armed with new spears, and the fight was on again. Finally, Alexander fell, wounded in the thigh; and Menelaus, hoping to take complete vengeance and win greatest glory, rushed forward to kill him. But Pandarus, committing an act of the blackest treachery by shooting his bow from a hidden spot, wounded Menelaus and caused him to halt. This stirred our men to wrath, and they raised a huge cry, feeling cheated because the Trojans had ended the fight in this treacherous way, especially this fight between the two men who had caused the whole war. During this general confusion, a group of barbarians rushed in and saved Alexander from danger.

|41| At the same time, Pandarus was taking advantage of our irresolution. Standing at a distance, he was finding many of our men with his arrows. He continued his slaughtering until Diomedes, stirred by this barbarous action, advanced upon him and cut him down at close quarters. Thus Pandarus, who had killed many men in violation of the treaty (that is, the agreement according to which Menelaus and Alexander should fight), paid with his life for his heinous method of fighting. His body was carried from the battle and duly cremated by Priam's sons; the ashes were given to his companions to take to Lycia for burial in his native soil.

Meanwhile the two armies had given the signal for battle and joined in combat. They fought until sundown with all their might, but neither side could claim a victory. With the coming of night, the commanders-in-chief withdrew their forces a short distance and posted sufficient guards along the facing battle lines.

They kept their men fully armed in these positions and waited for an opportunity to make a successful attack. But this opportunity never came, for winter began to set in, soaking the battlefield with frequent rains. The barbarians retreated within their walls, and our men, left with no enemy to fight, returned to the ships and took up winter duties. Dividing the portion of the plain that was unfit for battle into two parts, they cultivated the soil and grew whatever crops the time of year permitted.

During the same period, Ajax the son of Telamon, with a force consisting of his own men and some from the army of Achilles, made an attack against Phrygia, capturing cities and causing general destruction. Within a few days, he returned to camp, victoriously laden with booty.

|42| Just before his arrival, the barbarians made a sneak attack upon our men, who were relaxing in winter quarters and suspected no hostilities. Hector, the instigator of this rash expedition, was chosen as leader. At daybreak, after calling all of his men to arms, he led them through the gates, with orders to move at

double-time straight for the ships, and fall upon us. Our forces, which were scattered hither and yon, were caught off guard. The flight of those who were attacked first increased the confusion of the others and made it difficult for them to arm. A great slaughter ensued. As soon as our men in the center gave way, Hector was at the ships, raging with firebrands and setting fire to the prows. None of us dared to oppose him. Our unforeseen plight frightened us almost to death, and we begged Achilles for help; but even now he refused. How suddenly and radically the spirit had changed in us and our enemies!

|43| But when Ajax the son of Telamon returned and learned where Hector was at the ships, he presented himself at this spot, dressed in his marvelous armor. There he was, streaming with sweat, his great bulk pressing against the enemy, as he drove them away from the ships and thrust them outside the rampart. The more they retreated, the more he pressed his attack.

Hector, however, stood his ground—too bold for his own good, for Ajax struck him with a huge rock and sent him sprawling. Then, from every direction, a large number of Trojans rushed up and, crowding around, rescued Hector out of the battle and carried him into the city, a hero half dead, his expedition a failure.

Ajax, being thus deprived of honor and glory, was all the more savage. Accompanied by Diomedes, Idomeneus, and the other Ajax, he pursued the Trojans, who fled pell-mell in terror. He was using his spear to hit those in the distance, his shield to crush those he met at close quarters. No one in that part of the battlefield escaped without wounds. Glaucus, the son of Hippolochus, Sarpedon, and Asteropaeus tried to stem their fearful route but, after briefly resisting, soon gave way, seriously wounded. The loss of these leaders caused the barbarians to lose all hope and, breaking ranks, they rushed for the gates in confusion. The passageway, however, was too narrow for the great number of men who tried to enter; they stumbled and fell, like a landslide, over each other. Ajax and the Greeks we just mentioned were soon upon them, and great numbers of barbarians, being terrified and confused, were cut down and killed. Among those who were slain were the sons of Priam, Antiphus and Polites, Pammon and Mestor, and the son of Troezenus, Euphemus, the Ciconians' glorious leader.

|44| Thus the arrival of Ajax caused the fortunes of war to change; the Trojans, until then victorious, lost their leaders, and were forced to pay for their ill-considered aggression. When evening came and the signal was given for retreat, our men returned to the ships, rejoicing in victory.

Then Agamemnon gave a dinner in honor of Ajax, at which time he praised this hero most highly and gave him beautiful gifts. Our other leaders, too, praised the courage of Ajax. No one was silent. They told of his valorous deeds, how he had captured and plundered many Phrygian cities, and how he had fought with Hector at the very ships, a battle to be remembered, and freed the ships from fire. There was no one who doubted that at that time, because of his many excellent and glorious deeds, all of our hopes for a successful campaign rested with him.

Within a short time Epeus repaired the two ships that had caught fire; only their prows had been destroyed.

Then the Greeks felt free to relax without fear, thinking that the Trojans, in view of the attack that had recently failed, would refrain from another attempt.

|45| During this time Rhesus, the son of Eion, arrived with a large army of Thracians; he had had some dealings with Priam who had promised him pay for his aid. On the day of his arrival, he waited until nightfall on the peninsula which adjoined his kingdom in Thrace. Then, about the time of the second watch, he advanced onto the Trojan plain, spread out his tents, and set up camp.

Diomedes and Ulysses, who were guarding this sector, having noticed the commotion from afar, thought that Priam was sending some Trojans on a reconnaissance mission. Accordingly, they seized their arms and, moving stealthily and looking all around as they went, soon arrived at the spot. There they discovered the Thracian guards, who, being wearied by their long journey, had fallen asleep. After killing these, they entered Rhesus' tent and slew the king himself. They were, however, afraid to press their luck any further, and so returned to the ships, taking along Rhesus' chariot and richly caparisoned horses. Then, having gone to their huts, they slept for the rest of the night.

At daybreak they went to all of our leaders and told about their successful adventure. The consensus was that the death of Rhesus would anger the Thracians and that they would make an attack. Therefore, everyone was ordered to stand by his arms and be ready for battle.

|46| We had not long to wait, for the Thracians, when they awoke, discovered that their king had been foully slain within his tent and saw the tell-tale traces the stolen chariot had left. Immediately, undisciplined and disorganized bands of men began rushing toward the ships. As soon as our men caught sight of the Thracians, they advanced, following their leader's commands, in a solid front. The two Ajaxes led the way; they were the first to meet and slay the enemy. Then our other leaders, in their various positions, cut down those who opposed them. Sometimes several of them united their strength to break the power of the attacking bands, and thus they slaughtered them, scattered and leaderless; no one survived.

As soon as these attackers had been wiped out, our men, obeying the signal to advance, hastened to the Thracian tents. The only Thracians still alive were those who had been left to guard the camp. When these saw our men advancing, they were

terrified and, abandoning everything, fled to the walls for safety.
It was really pathetic. Our men moved in from all sides and seized
the armor, horses, and royal wealth that fate had kindly left us.
|47| Thereupon, with Rhesus and his Thracians completely de-
stroyed, our forces returned to the ships, victoriously laden with
booty. Meanwhile the Trojans were frightened, as they watched
from their battlements, but to no avail for their ally, and
stayed within their walls. Their spirits broken by recent reverses,
they sent us envoys begging for peace. And thus a treaty was
made which both sides, making due sacrifice, swore to uphold.

At about the same time, Chryses (who was the priest of the
Sminthian Apollo, as we have said above) came to the Greeks to
thank them for returning his daughter, Astynome. Because of
this kindness, and because he knew that his daughter had been
properly treated, he was now bringing her back for Agamemnon
to have.

The next event was the return of Philoctetes from Lemnos,
along with those who had gone to take him his share of the booty.
He was still rather sick and walked with difficulty.

|48| Then our leaders held a meeting of the council, at which
Ajax the son of Telamon, having gone to the center, delivered
a speech. He advised us to send suppliants to Achilles to beg him,
on behalf of the officers and common soldiers, to give up his
wrath and resume his position of honor among us. We should,
he felt, act now, for now, in view of our recent victory and the
favorable treaty we had made, we would be seeking him out, not
because of our need, but merely to honor him as he deserved; we
wanted him with us, simply because of his greatness. Furthermore,
Ajax implored, Agamemnon should show his willingness to be
reconciled with Achilles. In their present circumstances, fighting,
as they were, this terrible war in a far-off country, everyone should
think only of the common cause.

When he had finished speaking, all of our leaders agreed

unanimously with what he had said and praised him to the skies. He was, they said, not only stronger but also more intelligent than anyone else.

Then Agamemnon told how he had already sent many suppliants to try to reconcile Achilles. There was nothing he would more desire. Accordingly, he asked Ajax (whose relationship with Achilles should add to his persuasiveness) and Ulysses to undertake this mission and go to Achilles in behalf of them all.

Ajax and Ulysses promised to do what they could. And Diomedes offered to go along too.

|49| Thereupon Agamemnon ordered two attendants to bring a sacrificial victim. These brought the victim and held it above the ground while he, drawing his sword, cut it in half; the pieces fell to earth where all could see. This done, he walked through the middle, smearing his sword with blood. It was at this time that Patroclus, who had learned that the council was meeting, arrived. When Agamemnon had passed through the sacrifice, he swore that he had never violated Hippodamia; he had never been prone to lust or sensual pleasures; it was, rather, his inability to control his temper that had caused him countless troubles and brought him to this pass. Now he wanted to make the following offer: he would give Achilles one of his daughters to marry, whichever one he desired, besides a tenth of all his kingdom and fifty talents as dowry.

Those at the council, on hearing this, were amazed at his magnanimity. Patroclus was especially impressed by the offer of so much wealth, and he was also happy that Hippodamia had not been violated. Thus he returned to Achilles and told him all that had happened at the council.

|50| Achilles was pondering Agamemnon's offer, trying to decide what he should do, when Ajax and the other leaders entered his hut. He received them hospitably and offered them seats.

Ajax, having taken the seat that was next to Achilles, began, when the time seemed right, to chide and admonish him. Since they were relatives, he could speak more freely than the others. He blamed Achilles for nursing his wrath when many of his friends and most of his relatives—they, his people, were in serious danger—were begging him to relent.

Ulysses was next to speak. First, he said that the gods were to blame for what had happened so far. Then he told about the meeting of the council, about the promises Agamemnon had made and the oath Agamemnon had taken. Finally, urging Achilles not to scorn the prayers of the Greeks and not to spurn such a marriage, he ended by listing all of the dowry that Agamemnon was offering.

|51| Then Achilles, in a long speech, began by expounding upon his deeds and accomplishments, reminding them of the many labors he had borne for the common good, of the cities he had stormed. While everyone else was relaxing, he had spent his days and nights anxiously and zealously committed to war, sparing neither himself nor his soldiers; and, furthermore, he had allowed the booty he had carried off to be distributed among the entire army. In return for these services, he had received the unique honor of being deprived of his just reward. Only he had been treated with such contempt, such dishonor, for he had been robbed of Hippodamia, his prize, the symbol of his success. Agamemnon was not entirely to blame. What was even worse, all the other Greek leaders, forgetful of past kindnesses, had, by keeping silent, ignored the fact that he was being insulted.

When Achilles had finished speaking, Diomedes said: "What is past is past, and a wise man does not dwell upon it. Try as you may, you can not call it back."

Meanwhile Phoenix and Patroclus were standing around Achilles in the position of suppliants, taking hold of his knees and, without restraint, kissing his hands and face, begging him to give up his wrath and return to his place of honor. Do this, they said, not so much for these representatives but, as is right, for all of the army.

|52| Finally Achilles yielded.[16] He would do what they wanted. The sight of the representatives, the prayers of his closest friends, and the realization that the army was not to blame had made him change his mind.

Then for the first time after his wrath, at the suggestion of Ajax, Achilles went to a meeting of the council. Agamemnon greeted him in a royal manner, and the other leaders were happy to welcome him back. On every side there was joy, unbounded joy. And then Agamemnon, taking Achilles by the hand, led him off, along with the other leaders, to dinner.

A little later, during the dinner, when they were enjoying themselves, Agamemnon commanded Patroclus to take Hippodamia to Achilles' hut, and also the jewelry he had given to her. This was an order Patroclus was glad to obey.

During this winter, Greeks and Trojans mingled in the grove of the Thymbraean Apollo.[17] They went freely, whether singly or in groups, without any fear of each other.

Book Three

|1| Both Greeks and Trojans kept the truce and refrained from hostilities throughout the whole winter. The Greeks took advantage of the break and spent all their time and energies preparing for battle. They would assemble in front of the rampart, under their various leaders, each in the contingent that practiced his specialty. One group would practice throwing the spear, using, as a rule, pikes of exactly the right weight and length, or else pointed stakes. Others would practice hurling the sling or shooting the bow. Among those excelling in archery were Ulysses, Teucer, Meriones, Epeus, and Menelaus; but Philoctetes was the best: he owned the bow of Hercules, and always hit the mark with amazing skill.

The Trojans and their allies were, in comparison with the Greeks, almost carefree. They feared no treachery, and therefore neglected their military duties, spending their time making frequent sacrifices to the Thymbraean Apollo.

At about the same time they were informed that almost all of the cities of Asia had turned against Priam and were breaking off diplomatic relations with Troy. These cities blamed Priam for upholding Alexander's cause: he was setting a bad example which would undermine the laws of friendship in their region. Also, they were well aware that the Greeks had won all their battles to date and had conquered many of the neighboring cities. Last but not least, they hated Priam's sons and Priam's kingdom.

|2| One day, at Troy, when Hecuba was praying to Apollo,

Achilles and a few of his men came to watch the religious ceremonies. Many other women were there besides Hecuba: her daughters-in-law, for instance, and the wives of the leading Trojans; some of these, in pure devotion to their queen, attended upon her, while others, pretending to be so devoted, had really come to pray for something for themselves. There were also the daughters of Hecuba, Polyxena and Cassandra, as yet unmarried. They were the priestesses of Minerva and Apollo. Their hair was disheveled, their fillets strange and barbarous. Polyxena was the one who had set them to these duties.

When Achilles by chance turned his gaze on Polyxena, he was struck by the beauty of the girl. The longer he remained there, the deeper his passion grew. Finding no relief, he returned to the ships and, after several days of increasing torment, sent for Automedon and laid bare his heart. Automedon, he finally begged, must go to Hector and plead his suit for the girl.

As for Hector, he, to be sure, would give him his sister to marry if he would betray the whole army to him.

|3| Accordingly, Achilles promised that he would bring the whole war to an end if Polyxena were given to him.

Then Hector said that Achilles must either swear an oath to this betrayal or kill the sons of Plisthenes and Ajax; and that otherwise he was going to hear of no agreement.

Achilles, on hearing this, became terribly angry and shouted that, in the first battle, as soon as fighting was resumed, he was going to kill Hector. Then, his heart being wounded by his violent emotion, he wandered around, now here, now there; sometimes, nevertheless, he considered how far he should go in meeting Hector's demands.

But when Automedon saw how violently he was disturbed and that, as the days went by, he was becoming more and more distraught with longing, and spending the nights outside his hut, he feared that Achilles might harm himself or the leaders mentioned above, and thus he revealed the whole matter to Patroclus and Ajax. These kept a careful watch on their friend, without letting on that they knew anything.

As it happened, in time Achilles came to his senses. Having summoned Agamemnon and Menelaus, he told them about his love for Polyxena and about his dealings with Hector. Then everyone tried to console him by pointing out that the girl would be his soon enough, for, before very long, force would succeed where entreaty had failed.

What they said seemed reasonable, since the fall of Troy was already imminent: all the cities of Asia had broken off diplomatic relations with Priam and had willingly offered their aid and alliance to us. Our leaders had answered politely: Our present forces were quite sufficient, and we had no need of auxiliaries; though, to be sure, we willingly accepted the friendship they offered, and their good will would be pleasing to us. This we said, no doubt, because their faith was not to be trusted, their courage was too little tested, and their sudden change of allegiance was probably made with guile.

|4| Winter came to an end and, with the beginning of spring, both Greeks and Trojans were ready for war. They called their forces to arms and, giving the signal, led them onto the plain. When they had advanced, in formation, close enough to use their spears, they raised the war cry and joined in battle. The cavalry on both sides held the center and were therefore first to clash: the kings ascended their chariots and entered the fray, each beside the charioteer he had chosen to guide his horses.

Diomedes was in the van. Bearing down upon Pyraechmes, the king of the Paeonians, he slew him with a spear-thrust in the face. The retainers of Pyraechmes, men he had chosen because of their courage, banded together and tried to resist. But Diomedes, riding through their midst at full gallop, ran some of them down with his chariot and put the others to flight with his spear.

Then Idomeneus (Meriones was his charioteer) killed Acamas, the king of the Thracians. Thrusting him out of his chariot, he caught him, as he fell, on the tip of his spear.

When Hector, who was fighting in another part of the plain, heard that the Trojan horsemen in the center were fleeing, he ran to their rescue, leaving his command in the hands of worthy fighters, and taking along Glaucus, Deiphobus, and Polydamas. Without a doubt, the Trojans in the center would have been completely destroyed if Hector had not arrived and checked their flight. Now we were no longer able to mop them up, our offensive was dead; nevertheless, we held our ground and refused to retreat before Hector and the other recent arrivals.

|5| Soon news of this battle spread throughout the army, and the other leaders, having entrusted their positions to worthy subordinates, rushed toward the center. The battle lines, on both sides, were closed up, and the battle was renewed. Hector felt greatly encouraged, seeing that a large number of Trojans were present and thinking himself sufficiently safe. Then he urged on his men to fight with more daring, shouting in a loud voice and calling them each by name; and he himself entered the battle and wounded the two brave leaders of the Elians, Diores and Polyxenus.

As soon as Achilles saw Hector attacking like this, he came to the aid of the embattled Greeks, his spirit moved by the thought of how Hector had rejected his suit for Polyxena. He was forced, however, to stop in mid-course and slay Pylaemenes, the king of the Paphlagonians, who stood in his way. Pylaemenes, so they say, claimed to be related to Priam through Phineus, the son of Agenor, for Phineus' daughter, Olizone, on coming of age, had been married to Dardanus.[1]

|6| Then Achilles continued his raging drive against Hector, but Hector, who knew very well how hateful he was to Achilles, refused to stay where he was and, mounting his chariot, fled from

the battle. Achilles pursued as far as the enemy lines and, throwing his spear, mortally wounded Hector's charioteer, after Hector had abandoned his horses and escaped to another sector. Achilles was terribly vexed when he thought how the man he most hated had eluded his grasp. After extracting his spear from the charioteer, he raged all the more violently, slaying all who opposed him, trampling, as he advanced, over the dead.

The Trojans fled, terrified, until Helenus, who had found a distant hiding place from which to shoot his arrow, put an end to Achilles' attack. Achilles was caught off guard. His hand was hit, and thus the great champion of the Greeks, he who had caused Hector to flee in fear, he who had slain many men and their leaders, was forced from the field, treacherously wounded.

|7| Meanwhile Agamemnon and the two Ajaxes, amidst their general slaughter of insignificant opponents, caught and slew many of Priam's sons. Agamemnon slew Aesacus and Deiopites and also Archemachus, Laudocus, and Philenor. The Ajaxes—both the son of Oileus and the Telamonian Ajax—slew Mylius, Astynous, Doryclus, Hippothous, and Hippodamas.

In another part of the field Patroclus and Sarpedon the Lycian had withdrawn from their men and were trying to protect the flanks of their respective armies. Driving out beyond the battle lines, they challenged each other to fight in single combat. First, they threw their spears, but neither hit the mark. Then, leaping from their chariots and drawing their swords, they came face to face and fought for much of the day, exchanging blows fast and furious, but neither could wound the other. Finally, Patroclus, realizing that he must act with greater boldness, crouched behind the protection of his shield and came to close quarters. With his right hand he dealt Sarpedon a crippling blow along the back sinews of the leg and then, pressing his body against him—Sarpedon was faint and beginning to totter—pushed him over and finished him off as he fell.

|8| The Trojans, seeing what had happened, cried aloud and abandoned their battle formation, and, at a given signal, made a concerted attack against Patroclus. They felt, no doubt, that Sarpedon's death was a general disaster for their side. Patroclus, however, had seen the enemy coming. Protected by his armor and holding a spear he had snatched from the ground, he resisted more boldly. He slew Gorgythion and drove off Deiphobus, Gorgythion's brother, wounding him in the leg with his spear. Soon afterwards Ajax arrived and put the other Trojans to flight.

At about the same time Hector, who had also learned what was happening, came to the rescue. He rebuked the Trojan officers and stopped most of the men from retreating. He made them turn and resume, for the time, their battle formation. Thus by his presence he restored the spirits of his people and caused the battle to be renewed. The battle lines clashed, both sides being inspired by marvelous leaders. Now these were attacking, now those. Wherever the lines seemed about to give way, reinforcements came up. Meanwhile both armies were losing great numbers of men, and victory was favoring neither. When evening came, after a long and increasingly wearisome day of intensive fighting, the soldiers on both sides were glad to depart from the battle.

|9| Then Troy was filled with cries of grief. All the Trojans, especially the women, were weeping and wailing around the body of Sarpedon. They felt that no other disaster, however bitter, could be compared with this, not even the deaths of Priam's sons. They had believed in Sarpedon. They had hoped that he would protect them. But now their hopes were dashed.

The Greeks, for their part, returning to camp, immediately went to Achilles. After inquiring about his wound and learning, to their joy, that he was not suffering, they told him about the brave deeds of Patroclus. Then, before scattering to their different huts, they visited and inspected all the others who were wounded.

When Patroclus returned, Achilles praised him and urged

that the memory of what he had done that day should spur him to fight more fiercely in future battles.

Thus Trojans and Greeks spent this night. When dawn arrived, they collected, cremated and buried their dead. Then, after some days, when the wounded were well, they readied their arms and drew up their forces for battle.

|10| The barbarians, in accordance with their utter lack of principles, began hostilities with a sneak attack. Pitched battles were not to their liking; nothing else than treachery and turmoil would do. They fell upon us like a landslide, hurling their javelins with barbarous war cries. Many of our men, being caught off guard and half-armed, were killed, including Arcesilaus, the Boeotian, and Schedius, the Crissaean, both of whom were the best of leaders. The number of the wounded, however, was even greater; among whom were Meges, the ruler of the Echinades, and Agapenor, ruler of Arcadia.

During this terrible conflict, Patroclus, seeing our side being beaten, hoped he could turn the tide of battle. Thus, having exhorted our men, he entered the fray and attacked the enemy fiercely, more fiercely than anyone ever. Euphorbus, however, found him with a javelin. And soon Hector rushed up and, straddling the fallen body, dealt it many piercing thrusts and then tried to drag it from the battle. No doubt, in keeping with his people's total lack of human decency, Hector wanted to mock and mangle this victim in every way.

When Ajax, who was fighting in another part of the field, saw what was happening, he came up quickly; using his spear, he drove off Hector, who was already beginning to drag the body away. Meanwhile Menelaus and the other Ajax were pouncing upon Euphorbus and making him pay with his life for having been the cause of Patroclus' death. When evening finally came and the battle was broken off, a great number of our men were dead, treacherously and barbarously slain.

|11| Now that the two armies had withdrawn, we were free to relax. Our leaders went to Achilles. He was showing every sign of unbearable grief, for his face was distorted with weeping as he lay stretched out on the ground or over the body. He stirred everyone's heart. Even Ajax, who was standing by and trying to console him, broke down and wept. All of our leaders bewailed the death of Patroclus and, even more, the terrible way he had been mutilated; this was the first instance of such a shameful and inhuman act, a thing that the Greeks had never practiced before. Thus our leaders, with many prayers, consoling Achilles in every way, finally persuaded him to arise. Then, having washed the body of Patroclus, they covered it with a robe, being especially careful to hide the wounds, which to behold caused them to weep.

|12| When this had been done, Achilles exhorted the guards to keep careful watch in case the enemy should make an attack in their usual way, while we were detained with the burial. Accordingly, the guards, each of whom was dedicated to his duty, armed themselves and spent the night keeping the watchfires burning brightly.

At daybreak, since we had decided to hold a public funeral, we chose five of the leaders, Ialmenus, Ascalaphus, Epeus, Meriones, and the other Ajax, to go to Mount Ida for wood. Then we built a huge pyre with the wood which they brought, in a place five spears long and five spears wide, which Ulysses and Diomedes had measured off. After the body had been arranged, we lit the fire. Patroclus was clothed in the most beautiful and costly garments; Hippodamia and Diomedea (he had loved her especially) had seen to this.

|13| After spending a few days catching up on their sleep, our leaders early one morning led forth our army onto the plain. We waited and waited, but the barbarians, looking from their walls and seeing us armed, would not come out and fight. Therefore, at sunset we returned to the ships.

The next day, however, had hardly begun when the Trojans armed themselves and rushed from their gates, hoping, as was their custom, to catch us off guard with a wild and sudden attack. But we were organized well enough to protect ourselves, and, therefore, their javelins, which they, as they came against our fortifications, hurled in great numbers with energy and spirit, usually failed of their mark. Towards the end of the day we noticed that they were showing signs of strain and losing some of their fierceness. Accordingly, those of our men who were facing their left flank went on the offensive and thus scattered and put them to flight. Soon afterwards the other flank, which was already wavering, was driven off without any trouble.

|14| Turning tail, most of them fled like shameless cowards; and we, pursuing and treading them down, slew great numbers; among whom were the rulers of Larissa, Pylaeus and Hippothous, and the ruler of Sestos, Asius, the son of Hyrtacus. On the same day, Diomedes took twelve captives; Ajax took forty. Two of the captives, Pisus and Evander, were sons of Priam. As for the casualties on our side in this battle, Guneus, the king of the Cyphians, was slain, and my leader, Idomeneus, was wounded.

When the Trojans had reached the safety of their walls and shut the gates, we were no longer able to pursue. Remembering the outrage that had been committed against the body of Patroclus, we stripped the enemy corpses of their armor and dumped them into the river. Then we gave all the captives to Achilles, one after the other, as we had captured them.

Achilles, having doused the ashes of Patroclus with wine, gathered the remains into an urn. He intended to carry them, whenever he went, to his native soil, or be buried with them, with his dearest friend, there in the self-same tomb if fate decreed his death. He ordered the captives we had given him, including the sons of Priam, to be led off to the pyre and slaughtered not far from the ashes, no doubt as a sacrifice to the departed spirit of Patroclus.

Then he threw the bodies of the sons of the king to the dogs to be torn apart. He swore that he would spend his nights under the open sky until he had taken vengeance, blood for blood, on the man who was the cause of his unspeakable grief.

|15| After a few days news was suddenly brought that Hector and a few other men had set out to meet Penthesilea, the queen of the Amazons.[2] Why she was coming to Priam's aid, whether for money or simply because of her love of war, was uncertain; her race, being naturally warlike, was always conquering the neighboring peoples and carrying the Amazon standards far and wide. Accordingly, Achilles chose a few faithful comrades and hastened to lay an ambush for the Trojans. He caught them off guard—they were trying to cross a river—and surrounded and slew them before they knew what had hit them. Hector and all those who were with him were killed; with the single exception of one of Priam's sons, whom Achilles captured and, having cut off his hands, sent back to Troy to tell what had happened. Achilles was being driven to bestial acts, first by the slaughter of his most hated enemy, and then by his lasting grief for Patroclus. Having stripped Hector of armor, he tied the body, feet bound together, behind his chariot, then mounted and ordered Automedon, his charioteer, to give the horses free reins. And so he went galloping over the plain where he could be most easily seen dragging his enemy. A new and terrible kind of revenge.

|16| But at Troy, the Trojans, looking down from their walls, saw the armor of Hector, which Achilles had ordered the Greeks to carry within sight of the enemy. And the son of Priam whom Achilles had sent back told what had happened. Throughout the whole city there was weeping and wailing; in answer to which our men shouted insults. The noise was so loud that even the birds seemed to fall from the sky, dumbfounded, confused. All the gates of the city were closed. The kingdom, dressed in mourning, hid its face in woe. As often happens in such circumstances, the

frenzied people would suddenly rush to one place and then, for no apparent reason, rush off again in all directions. Now there was shrieking everywhere; now an uncanny and total silence. Many of the Trojans were losing all hope. They thought that, with the coming of night, the Greeks, elated at the death of Hector, would make an attack against the walls and take the city by storm. Some of them believed that the army which Penthesilea had brought to aid Priam was now joined with Achilles; everything was adverse and hostile, all their power was broken and destroyed. They had no hope of safety, for Hector was dead. He alone had ever been an equal match for the countless hordes, for the many leaders of the enemy. His valor in battle was famed throughout the world and, nevertheless, it had not surpassed his wisdom.

|17| Meanwhile, among the Greeks, Achilles had brought the body of Hector back to the ships and shown it to everyone; the sorrow that we had recently felt for the death of Patroclus was replaced by exuberant joy over the slaughter of our formidable enemy. Since now there was nothing to fear from the Trojans, everyone was eager to hold games, as is customary at funerals, in honor of Patroclus.[3] The other peoples, moveover, who had come to watch and not participate, stood ready in arms to meet any attack the enemy, though broken in strength, might make in the usual treacherous way. Then Achilles ordered prizes to be set for the victors, things that he deemed of highest value. When everything was ready, he took a position in the midst of the kings, a little higher than the rest, and urged them all to take their seats.

In the first contest, the four-horse chariot race, Eumelus was victor. No one could beat him. Diomedes won the prize in the two-horse chariot race. Menelaus came in second.

|18| Next was the contest in archery. Ulysses and Meriones erected two masts between which, tied to the tops, they stretched a very thin cord, from the middle of which they hung a dove attached by a string. This was the target. Then all the contestants

took their turns. But only Ulysses and Meriones hit the mark. They were congratulated by everyone, except Philoctetes who boasted that he could do better: he would cut the string by which the dove was suspended. Our leaders marveled at the difficulty of what he was trying to do. Nevertheless, he, trusting in his skill more than in luck, made good his boast. The string was snapped and the dove fell to earth. A loud shout of approval arose from our men. Meriones and Ulysses received the prizes for this contest, but Achilles rewarded the exceptional feat of Philoctetes with a double prize.

|19| Ajax the son of Oileus won the long-distance race. Polypoetes came in second. Machaon won the double-lap race, Eurypylus the single-lap, Tlepolemus the high jump, and Antilochus the discus.

The prizes for wrestling went unawarded. Ajax had almost beaten Ulysses, gripping him by the waist and throwing him down. But Ulysses, even while falling, had entangled the feet of his opponent and knocked him off balance. Thus both men were sprawled on the ground.

The same Ajax, the son of Telamon, carried off the palm in all of the boxing matches, including the fight with the cestus.

Diomedes won the last contest, the race in full armor.

After Achilles had awarded the prizes, he gave gifts; first, the gift he thought was most valuable to Agamemnon; then to Nestor, to Idomeneus, to Podalirius and Machaon, and to all the other leaders in order of their merit; and finally, to the comrades of those who had fallen in battle, commanding them to take the gifts home, when time allowed, to the relatives of the deceased. By the time that the games were completed and the prizes awarded, it was already evening and everyone went to his hut.

|20| At daybreak Priam came to Achilles—a wretched sight, dressed in clothes of mourning, with suppliant face and suppliant hands, a king to whom grief had left no signs of royal majesty or

former power and glory.⁴ With him came Andromache, no less
wretched than himself, her features marred in every way. To aid
the king in his request, she brought her sons, leading them before
her, two little boys, Astyanax (some called him Scamandrius)
and Laodamas. And Polyxena also came, supporting her father,
as he tottered beneath the burden of his years and sorrows. Carts
followed, filled with gold and silver and costly clothing. This is
the picture of king and retinue that caused a sudden silence among
the astonished Trojans watching from their walls.

Soon our leaders were going to meet Priam, eager to discover
why he was coming. When Priam saw them advancing, he fell on
his face and threw dust, and whatever filth he could find, over
his head. He begged them to pity his fortunes and plead his case
with Achilles.

His old age and ruined life evoked the sympathy of Nestor.
Ulysses, however, cursed him, reminding him of how he had
spoken against the envoys at Troy before the war had begun.

When Achilles learned of Priam's arrival, he sent Automedon to summon the king. He himself waited, holding the urn
that contained the bones of Patroclus.

|21| Accordingly, Priam, along with our leaders, entered the hut
of Achilles. Then, clasping Achilles' knees, he said: "You are not
to blame for my misfortunes. It is one of the gods who, instead of
pitying me, has brought the end of my life to ruin. Now I am
overwhelmed and worn out with grief for my sons. They, con-
fident in their youth and the resources of their kingdom, and
always desiring to fulfill the desires of their hearts, have devised,
contrary to their expectations, destruction both for themselves
and for me. It is their maxim that old age should be despised by
youth. Nevertheless, if my death will prevent those of my sons
who are left from committing other crimes of this sort, I also offer
myself, if thus it is pleasing, for capital punishment. Do as you
wish. With one stroke take away my little life and all those tribulations which have made me a sorrowful wretch, a most miserable

spectacle among men. Here I am. I ask no mercy. Take me captive, if you wish. Nothing remains of my former fortune; my kingdom fell when Hector died. But if I have already paid with my personal sorrows, with the blood of my sons, a sufficient penalty to all Greece for the ill-considered acts of my people, pity my age, consider the gods, remember piety. At least grant the petition of these young boys for the body, not the life, of their father, Hector. Remember your own father who is spending all of his waking hours thinking of you, wondering if you are safe. May all his prayers be answered. May he enjoy a good old age, one far different from mine."

|22| While he was talking, his spirit was failing. Then, as he lost his power of speech, his legs gave way. Everyone who was present was pained at this very pitiable sight.

Then Andromache prostrated the small sons of Hector before Achilles. She herself was weeping; with a voice full of sorrow, she begged for permission only to look at the body of her husband.

During this pitiable scene, Phoenix was raising Priam and encouraging him to recover. When the king had revived somewhat, he spoke, while kneeling and pulling his hair with both hands: "Where is that righteous mercy for which the Greeks were famous? Is it denied to Priam alone?"

|23| Everyone was deeply moved. Achilles, however, said that Priam should have prevented his sons from their criminal acts in the beginning. By acquiescing, he had become their accomplice in treachery. Ten years ago he was not so old that they would have refused to listen to him. But, as it was, their greed, their lust for the property of others, had driven them to monstrous acts: they had carried off not only a woman but also the wealth of Atreus and Pelops. It was simple justice that they should receive their present punishments, or even worse. Until now, the Greeks had obeyed civilized rules of war and returned the bodies of their enemies for burial. But Hector had acted contrary to the laws of human nature when he dragged the body of Patroclus from the

battle, with the evident intent of abusing and defiling it. Now the Trojans must bear their punishments in expiation of this crime. Thus, in future time, the Greeks and other peoples, remembering what had happened in this case, would keep the natural law. The Greeks had not left their homes and children and come to fight this bloody, toilsome war just for Helen's sake, or Menelaus'. What they really wanted to decide was who would rule the world, themselves or the barbarians. Nevertheless, the abduction of a woman was cause enough for an invasion: those who are plundered grieve over their losses no less than the plunderers delight in their gains. So saying, Achilles called down curses upon Helen, swearing that when Troy was taken he would slay her in public, a fitting reward for her crime. He blamed her for his loss of native land and parents and, also, of the greatest consolation of his homesick heart, Patroclus.

|24| Then Achilles stood up and went out to consult with the leaders mentioned above. He was persuaded to follow their unanimous advice: he would accept the gifts that were being offered and hand over the body of Hector. When this had been decided, the leaders departed to their different huts, and he returned to his.

Upon his reentry, Polyxena fell at his feet and promised to be his willing slave if he would return the body. This sight, and also the thought of father and son, moved him to tears, in spite of all of his hatred for Priam and Troy because of Patroclus' death. Thus he gave Polyxena his hand and helped her to rise; but first he showed his concern for Priam and commanded Phoenix to comfort him. When, however, Priam refused to be consoled and continued to lament, Achilles swore that Priam's wishes would not be satisfied until he had changed into better clothes and dined with him. And so the king, fearing to refuse, lest he lose what seemed to have been granted, decided humbly to submit to the will of Achilles.

|25| After shaking the dust from his hair, he took a bath; and

then he and his retinue went to dine with Achilles. When everyone had had enough to eat, their host spoke as follows: "Now tell me, Priam, what was the real reason you thought Helen should be kept so long, even when your military efforts were failing and your troubles and tribulations were steadily mounting? Why did you not drive her out, like an ill-omened plague? You knew that she had betrayed her native land and parents and, what was most disgraceful, her god-like brothers.[5] These brothers cursed her crime and refused even to join with us in this campaign, lest, to be sure, they should be responsible for obtaining her return. Why, when she had come to Troy to be a bane to everyone, why did you not throw her out? Why did you not drive her from your walls with curses? Why did the elders of Troy acquiesce when their sons were dying every day in battle? Could it be that they did not know that she alone was causing all those deaths? Is everyone in Troy so demonically infatuated that no one can be found to pity the failing fortunes of his country and try to save her with the death of Helen? For my part, I honor both your old age and your prayers. I shall return the body. Never shall I allow myself to be guilty of crimes I condemn in my enemies."

|26| These words made Priam begin to weep again. He said that it had been the will of the gods for him to go to war. The gods were the authors of good and evil for every mortal; so long as he had been permitted to be happy, the might of none of his enemies had succeeded against him. He who had fathered fifty sons by different mothers had been considered the most blessed of all kings, until the birth of the youngest, Alexander. He had been unable to avoid the future, even though the gods had revealed the events that Alexander would cause. When Hecuba was pregnant, she had told him how she had dreamt of a torch in whose flames Mount Ida and then, as the fire continued, the shrines of the gods and finally the whole state had been consumed, excepting only the homes of Antenor and Anchises. The interpreters had said that this dream portended the fall of Troy. Accordingly, they had de-

cided to kill the baby at birth. But Hecuba, with a woman's tenderness toward her child, had given him secretly to shepherds to rear on Mount Ida. When he was grown, and they knew what had happened, he was so handsome that no one, not even his fiercest enemy, could bear to kill him. Then he had married Oenone. Soon, however, having been seized with a desire of seeing faraway regions and kingdoms, he had gone on that journey on which he carried off Helen; some god was urging him, driving him on. As for Helen, all the Trojans, including Priam himself, loved her. Not even the thought of the deaths of their sons and relatives could persuade them to reject her. Only Antenor, his wisest counselor in peace and war, was for this; Antenor, in the beginning, when Alexander returned from Greece, even disowned his own son, Glaucus, because he had gone along on that journey. Now Troy was being destroyed and he, the king, was near to death. In fact, he longed to die and give up the burden of being king. He was tortured only by the thought that when his country fell, Hecuba and his daughters would be enslaved. What masters, what shame, would they have to endure?

|27| When Priam had finished this speech, he ordered that everything be displayed which he had brought to ransom his son. Achilles commanded the gold and silver to be removed, and also the clothes he liked best. Having gathered together what was left, he gave it to Polyxena. Then he handed over the body to Priam. The king, whether desiring to show his gratitude for being able to hold the funeral, or hoping to insure the safety of his daughter if Troy should fall, fell at the knees of Achilles and begged him to take Polyxena and keep her for himself. The young man answered that she should return with her father; they would see about her at some other time and in some other place.

Thus Priam recovered the body of Hector and, mounting his chariot, returned to Troy along with the others.

Book Four

|1| On learning that the king had accomplished his mission and returned unharmed along with the others, the Trojans praised the Greeks' compassion. Priam, they had thought, would never obtain the body; the Greeks would feel justified in holding him prisoner since they, the Trojans, had refused to give Helen up.

When they saw Hector's body, everyone, including the allies, ran forward. They were weeping and pulling their hair and scratching their faces. The city was ruled by despair. Hector, whose deeds in war and peace alike were known throughout the world, his fame being due to his righteous character no less than to his martial spirit, Hector was dead. They buried him close to the tomb of their former king Ilus;[1] and, gathering around, on this side the women with Hecuba, on that the Trojan men and their allies, they raised the mournful dirge. For ten days from sunrise until sunset, the time of the truce, everyone, without ceasing, wailed for Hector, as was his due.

|2| During the funeral Penthesilea (whom we have mentioned above) arrived. She brought a huge army of Amazons and other neighboring peoples. On being informed of Hector's death, she was very upset and desired to go home. But Alexander gave her much gold and silver, and finally prevailed upon her to stay.

Several days later she drew up her forces and made an attack, without any help from the Trojans, so great was her trust in her people. She arranged the archers on the right flank, the foot soldiers on the left, and the cavalry, to which she herself belonged,

in the center. Our men were drawn up to meet her, with Menelaus, Ulysses, Meriones, and Teucer against the archers, the two
Ajaxes, Diomedes, Agamemnon, Tlepolemus, Ascalaphus, and
Ialmenus against the foot soldiers, and Achilles, along with the
others, against the cavalry. Thus the two armies, having drawn up
their forces, joined battle. The queen slaughtered many, using her
bow; as did Teucer for us. Meanwhile the Ajaxes were leading
the foot soldiers; advancing with their shields before them and
pushing back any who got in their way, they wreaked general
havoc; no one, it seemed, could stop them from wiping the enemy
out.

|3| Achilles found Penthesilea among the cavalry and, hurling
his spear, hit the mark. Then—no trouble now that she was
wounded—he seized her by the hair and pulled her off her horse.
Her followers, seeing her fallen, became disheartened and took
to flight. We pursued and cut down those who were unable to
reach the gates before they closed; nevertheless, we abstained
from touching the women because of their sex.

Then we returned, all of us victors, our enemies slain. Finding Penthesilea still half-alive, we marveled at her brazen boldness. Almost immediately a meeting was held to determine her
fate, and it was decided to throw her, while still alive enough to
have feeling, either into the river to drown or out for the dogs to
tear apart, for she had transgressed the bounds of nature and her
sex. Achilles favored just letting her die and then giving her
burial. Diomedes, however, prevailed: going around, he asked
everyone what to do and won a unanimous vote in favor of
drowning. Accordingly, dragging her by the feet, he dumped her
into the Scamander. It goes without saying that this was a very
cruel and barbarous act. But thus the queen of the Amazons,
having lost the forces she had brought to aid Priam, died in a
way that befitted her foolhardy character.

|4| On the following day, Memnon, the son of Tithonus and Aurora, arrived with a large army of Indians and Ethiopians, a truly remarkable army which consisted of thousands upon thousands of men with various kinds of arms, and surpassed the hopes and prayers even of Priam. All the country around and beyond Troy, as far as eye could see, was filled with men and horses, and glittered with the splendor of arms and standards. Memnon had led these forces to Troy by way of the Caucasus mountains.

At the same time he had sent another group of equal size by sea, with Phalas as their guide and leader. These others had landed on the island of Rhodes, which they soon discovered to be an ally of Greece. At first, fearing that when the purpose of their mission was known, their ships might be fired, they stayed in the harbor. Later, however, dividing their strength, they went to the wealthy cities of Camirus and Ialysus.

Soon the Rhodians were blaming Phalas for trying to aid Alexander, the same Alexander who had recently conquered Phalas' country, Sidon.[2] In order to stir up the army, they said that whoever defended this crime was in no way different from a barbarian; and they added many such things as would incense the common soldiers and make them take their side. Nor did they fail in their intent, for the Phoenicians, who composed a majority of Phalas' army, whether influenced by the accusations of the Rhodians, or wishing to gain control of the wealth their ships were carrying, made an attack against Phalas and stoned him to death. Then, dividing their gold and whatever booty they had, they dispersed to the cities we mentioned above.

|5| Meanwhile the army that had come with Memnon had set up camp in a wide area (the walls of the city could not have easily contained so great a number of men), and everyone, each in his own particular group, was training for combat. These groups differed in their fighting methods and skills according to the

regions from which they came. Their different kinds of weapons, their different kinds of shields and helmets, gave them a terrifying warlike appearance.

Then at dawn, after several days, when his soldiers were ready to fight, Memnon gave them the signal and led them to battle. And the Trojans, along with their allies, left the protection of their walls and also advanced. We, for our part, drew up our forces to meet them, being somewhat awed by the size of our unknown enemy. When they had come within a spear's throw of our side, they fell upon us with a huge and dissonant clamor. It was like a landslide. Our men, standing together, were able to break their attack. But soon their lines were renewed and reformed, and weapons were flying this way and that, and many on both sides were dying. Nor was there any end in sight, so long as Memnon, accompanied by all of his bravest men, was attacking our center, riding in his chariot, and slaying or wounding whomever he met. Our casualties were mounting terribly, and our leaders conceded defeat; they felt that we were destined to lose and that our only hope was in flight. But night, the refuge of the oppressed, kept the enemy off. Otherwise, that day would have seen our ships destroyed by fire; so great was Memnon's power and martial skill, so grievous our predicament.

|6| When the fighting had stopped, we, being broken in spirit and fearing the war's final outcome, spent the night burying those we had lost in battle. Then we thought of a plan: one of our men should challenge Memnon to fight in single combat. Accordingly, we proceeded to choose a champion by lot. The lots of all were shaken, excepting only—as Agamemnon requested—Menelaus', Ulysses', and Idomeneus'; and Ajax, the son of Telamon, in answer to everyone's prayers, was chosen. Then we ate and renewed our strength and spent the rest of the night in sleep.

At daybreak we armed, drew up our forces in order, and went out to battle. Memnon, no less alert, also advanced, and with him all the Trojans. When both of the armies were ready, the battle was joined. As might be expected, a great number of men fell dead on both sides, or withdrew mortally wounded. It was in this battle that Antilochus, the son of Nestor, ran into Memnon, and thus met his death.

When Ajax thought that the time was right, he went out between the lines and challenged the king. First, however, he called on Ulysses and Idomeneus to defend him in case any others attacked. Memnon, seeing Ajax advance, leaped from his chariot and met him on foot. Among both armies fear and hope were running high. Finally Ajax thrust his spear into the center of Memnon's shield and, using all his weight and force, shoved it through and into Memnon's side. The companions of Memnon, when they saw what had happened, rushed to his aid and tried to push Ajax away. But this interference on the part of the barbarians stirred Achilles to act; he entered the fray and drove his spear through Memnon's throat, where the shield gave no protection.

|7| Memnon's unexpected death, while breaking the enemy's spirit, bolstered ours. Now the Ethiopians had turned and were fleeing; now our men were pursuing, wreaking great slaughter. Polydamas tried to renew the battle, but soon was surrounded and fell, hit in the groin by Ajax. And Glaucus, the son of Antenor, was killed; he was fighting Diomedes when Agamemnon struck him down with a spear. One might see Ethiopians and Trojans fleeing everywhere over the field in disorder, without leaders, crowding and rushing, hindering each other, falling where driverless horses were trampling them down. Our men, their spirits renewed, were attacking and slaughtering the enemy, scattering those who had been entangled and then picking them off with their spears. The field near the walls was flowing with blood; armor and corpses abounded wherever the enemy went. It was in this battle that Priam lost the following sons: Aretus and Echem-

mon were killed by Ulysses; Dryops, Bias, and Chorithan³ were killed by Idomeneus; Ilioneus and Philenor by Ajax the son of Oileus; Thyestes and Telestes by Diomedes; Antiphus, Agavus, Agathon, and Glaucus by the other Ajax; and Asteropaeus by Achilles. There was no end to the slaughter until our men were finally thoroughly sated, thoroughly tired.

|8| When we had returned to camp, the Trojans sent envoys to obtain permission to bury their dead. Thus the dead were gathered, each by his own, and cremated and buried according to ancient custom. Memnon, however, was cremated apart from the others; his remains were put in an urn and given to relatives to take to his native land.⁴

When we had duly washed the body of Antilochus, we handed it over to Nestor for proper burial and begged him to bear the adversities of war with courage. Then, finally, each of us spent much of the night honoring his dead with wine and funeral feasts, and praising both Ajax and Achilles in highest terms.

The Trojans, with the completion of their funerals, ended their grief over Memnon's disaster. But now they were gripped by despair; they feared the war's final outcome. The death of Sarpedon and, soon afterwards, the slaughter of Hector, had taken away their remaining hopes; and now what fortune had for the last time offered in the person of Memnon no longer remained. Thus, with so many adversities conspiring against them, their will to recover was utterly gone.

|9| After a few days the Greeks took up arms and, having gone onto the field, challenged the Trojans to come out and fight, if they dared. Alexander and his brothers, in answer to this challenge, set their army in order and led it forth. But before the battle lines could meet or spears be thrown, the barbarians broke formation and took to flight. We rushed upon them, from this side and that, slaughtering great numbers, or hurling them headlong into the river; they had no way to escape. And two of Priam's sons were

captured, Lycaon and Troilus, the throats of whom, when they had been brought forth into the center, were cut, by order of Achilles, who was angry with Priam for not having seen to that business they had discussed. The Trojans raised a cry of grief and, mourning loudly, bewailed the fact that Troilus had met so grievous a death, for they remembered how young he was, who, being in the early years of his manhood, was the people's favorite, their darling, not only because of his modesty and honesty, but more especially because of his handsome appearance.

|10| After a few days, the religious festival of the Thymbraean Apollo began; a truce was made and hostilities ceased. Then, while both armies were preoccupied with sacrificing, Priam found time to send Idaeus to Achilles with instructions concerning Poly-xena. While, however, Achilles was examining these instructions, alone in the grove with Idaeus, word of this meeting was brought to the ships. Our men were angered, suspecting Achilles of being disloyal, for the rumor that he was a traitor had gradually grown and now was accepted as truth throughout the whole army. There-fore, in order to placate the fired-up emotions of the soldiers, Ajax, Diomedes and Ulysses went to the grove and stood in front of the temple, waiting for Achilles to leave. They likewise wanted to tell him what had happened at the ships and hoped to deter him from further secret dealings with Trojans.

|11| Meanwhile Alexander and Deiphobus, having formed a plot, approached Achilles, as if to confirm the agreement of Priam. In order to incur no suspicion, Alexander (he was wearing a dagger) stopped near the altar and faced away from our leader. Achilles was carrying no weapon, thinking there was nothing to fear in the temple of Apollo. Then Deiphobus, when the time seemed right, came up to Achilles and, with flattering congratulations for the terms he had made, embraced him and, hanging upon him, refused to let go until Alexander, with sword drawn, rushed forward and thrust two blows in the victim's sides. When they saw that he was

dying, they departed in haste and returned to the city, their very important mission accomplished beyond their fondest hopes.

Ulysses, who had seen them leave, said: "Something is wrong. Why are these men so excited? Why are they frightened and rushing like this?" And thereupon he and the others entered the grove and, looking around, discovered Achilles stretched on the ground, already half-dead with the loss of much blood.

Then Ajax said: "We know for a fact that no one could have defeated you in a fairly fought contest but, as is clear, you are undone by your own ill-advised rashness."

And Achilles, breathing his last, said: "Deiphobus and Alexander overpowered me. They came in the matter concerning Polyxena—deceitfully, treacherously."

As he lay there dying, our leaders embraced him and kissed him farewell. Great was their grief. And when he was dead, Ajax shouldered the body and carried it out of the grove.

|12| The Trojans, having seen what had happened, rushed from their gates all together. Following their usual custom, they wanted, no doubt, to mangle the body and thus were eager to snatch it away and carry it into the city. But the Greeks were also alerted and, taking up arms, advanced to meet them. Soon after they had led forth all of their forces, both sides clashed in battle.

Ajax, having handed the body of Achilles to those who were with him, went on the attack and slew Asius (the son of Dymas and the brother of Hecuba) whom he encountered first. Then he cut down a great number of others, as they came, one by one, within reach of his spear. Among these were Nastes and Amphimachus, the rulers of Caria.

And now our leaders, Ajax the son of Oileus and Sthenelus, joined together and killed and put great numbers to flight.

Finally this general destruction caused the Trojans to rush for their gates. They abandoned all hope of resisting and scattered and fled in utter disorder, believing that only their walls could

protect them. Behind them the Greeks were pursuing, piling
slaughter on slaughter.

|13| When the gates were closed and the slaughter had ended, the
Greeks took Achilles back to the ships. All of our leaders bewailed
the loss of this hero. Many of the soldiers, however, believing that
Achilles had often tried to betray them, were grieved not in the
least and refused to mourn as they should. Nevertheless, he had
been their greatest military asset and now, by his death, all was
lost. They had to admit that, for a man so outstanding in battle,
he had met a dishonorable death, or at least an obscure one.
Accordingly, they hastened to bring plenty of wood from Mount
Ida and built a pyre in the place where that of Patroclus had been.
Then, having put the body in place, they lit the fire, and thus performed the rites of the funeral. Ajax acted with special devotion,
keeping watch for three continuous days until the remains were
gathered together. He was grieved by the death of Achilles more
than any one else, grieved almost beyond his powers of endurance.
He had loved Achilles above all others and had served him with
highest allegiance, for Achilles was not only his relative and closest
friend but also, what especially mattered, the most courageous
man there was.

|14| The Trojans, for their part, abounded in joy and thanks-
giving, for the enemy whom they had feared the most was dead.
They lavished praises on Alexander's trickery; he had, to be sure,
done by devious means what he would never have dared to do in
combat.

Meanwhile a messenger arrived to tell Priam that Eurypylus,
the son of Telephus, was arriving from Mysia. (The king had
enticed him with many beautiful gifts, and had finally won his
support by offering Cassandra in marriage. Among the other very
beautiful things he had sent to him was a staff which, being made
of gold, was talked of far and wide.) Eurypylus, the illustrious
warrior, had come with his Mysian and Ceteian forces. The

Trojans welcomed him joyously, for in him their every hope was revived.

|15| Meanwhile the Greeks placed the bones of Achilles in an urn with those of Patroclus and buried the urn at Sigeum.[5] Then Ajax hired some Sigeans to build a tomb for Achilles; he was angry with the Greeks, for he thought that their grief was in no way equal to the loss of so great a hero.

When the tomb was almost finished, Pyrrhus arrived. He was called Neoptolemus and was the son of Achilles by Deidamia, the daughter of King Lycomedes. After being informed how his father had died, he reinforced the Myrmidons and bolstered their spirits; they were the bravest of men and famous in war. Then, leaving Phoenix in charge of this work, he went to the ships and there, at his father's hut, found Hippodamia guarding the property.

Soon his arrival was known, and all the leaders convened. When they begged him to keep control of himself, he, answering calmly, said that he knew well enough that men must bravely endure whatever the gods caused to happen. Everyone's life must come to an end; only the weak wanted old age, the strong shunned and despised it. Moreover, his grief was mitigated by the fact that Achilles had been killed neither in single combat nor in the blaze of war; Achilles could never have been beaten—it was unthinkable—by anyone, living or dead, with the single exception of Hercules. Though the time called for Achilles, under whose hands it was fitting that Troy should fall, nevertheless, he affirmed, they, with his help, would finish the task that his father had left uncompleted.

|16| After he had finished this speech, they decided to fight on the following day.

All of our leaders, when the time seemed right, went, as usual, to Agamemnon's to dine. Among them were Ajax and Neoptolemus, and Diomedes, Ulysses, and Menelaus; these took places of equal honor at dinner. While they were eating, they praised the prowess of Achilles and told Neoptolemus about the numerous brave deeds of his father. Their words delighted him and moved him to say that he would strive, with might and main, to prove himself a worthy son. After the dinner was over, they left to spend the night in their huts.

At dawn of the next day Neoptolemus, on leaving camp, was met by Diomedes and Ulysses. Having given them greeting, he asked if something was wrong. They answered that we should delay our attack a few days, until his soldiers recovered from their long journey by sea: their legs were still shaky, their feet were unsteady.

|17| And so, in accordance with this advice, our attack was delayed for two days. Then all our leaders and kings, having armed our men and set them in order, went out to battle. Neoptolemus commanded the center. With him were the Myrmidons and also Ajax (whom Neoptolemus, as befitted their close relationship, honored in place of his father).

The Trojans were very upset, for they saw that, while their own allies were daily defecting, a new contingent, led by an illustrious leader, had come to the aid of the Greeks. Nevertheless, they took up arms, as Eurypylus urged them to do. He, having gained the support of the princes, created a combined force consisting of his own men and those of the Trojans and, leading them out of the gate, deployed them for battle; he himself commanded the center. (Aeneas stayed behind in the city and, for the first time, refused to fight; he was a devoted worshiper of Apollo and detested the crime Alexander had committed against this god.)

When the signal for battle was given, the two sides clashed and fought with all their might; great numbers were slain. Eurypylus, chancing upon Peneleus, drove him back and pinned him with his spear; then he attacked Nireus even more savagely, and cut him down; and finally, having put to flight our men in front, he was fighting in the very midst of our forces. But Neoptolemus, on seeing this, drove up close and knocked Eurypylus out of his chariot; then he dismounted himself and, sword in hand, quickly finished Eurypylus off. Thereupon our men, as Neoptolemus ordered, carried the body out of the battle and back to the ships. When the barbarians—they had placed all their hopes in Eurypylus—saw this sight, they deserted the battle and fled for the walls, leaderless, without any definite order. And as they fled, great numbers were killed.

|18| Thus the enemy was put to flight, and the Greeks returned to the ships. Then, the council so willing, we cremated Eurypylus and sent his bones, in an urn, back to his father, for we remembered his father's kindness and friendship.[6] Also, there were separate funerals for Nireus and Peneleus; each was cremated by his own people.

On the next day Chryses reported to the Greeks that Priam's son Helenus had fled from Troy because of Alexander's crime and was now at the temple nearby. Accordingly, we sent Diomedes and Ulysses to fetch him. After these had promised him leave to spend the rest of his life somewhere in seclusion, he placed himself in their power.

When he had been brought to the ships, he made a long speech at a meeting of the council, in which he told his reason for leaving his parents and people: he feared not death but the gods, whose shrines Alexander had desecrated, a crime which neither Aeneas nor himself was able to bear. As for Aeneas, he, fearing our anger, had stayed behind with Antenor and old Anchises, his father. It was from an oracle of Anchises, Helenus said, that he had learned of Troy's imminent fall, and thus had made up his mind to come to us as a suppliant.

We were eager to know the contents of this oracle. Accordingly, Chryses, having nodded for us to keep silent, took Helenus aside and learned everything, which then he reported to us. Thus we were informed of the very time of Troy's fall and how Aeneas and Antenor would help us. And we saw that this oracle was entirely consistent with what we remembered Calchas had already told us was going to happen.

|19| On the next day both armies went out to battle and many were killed on the Trojan side, their allies suffering the greatest losses. But as our men were attacking more vehemently and striving with all their might to end the war, our leaders, at a given signal, attacked those of the enemy and centered the battle around themselves.

Philoctetes advanced against Alexander and challenged him to fight, if he dared, a duel with the bow. Alexander agreed, and thus Ulysses and Deiphobus marked off a place for the contest. Alexander was the first to shoot and missed. Thereupon Philoctetes hit Alexander in the left hand, and then—he was howling with pain—struck his right eye, and then—he was trying to flee— pierced both his feet, and finally finished him off. Philoctetes' arrows had once been Hercules', and the Hydra's lethal blood had stained their points.[7]

|20| The barbarians, seeing that their leader was dead, rushed in and tried to snatch his body away. Philoctetes killed many of them, but they kept pressing on, and eventually got the body into the city. Ajax the son of Telamon pursued them as far as the gate, and there the slaughter was huge. Many were unable to enter; the crowd was frantic, with everyone shoving, everyone striving to get in first. Those who had entered went to the walls and hurled down rocks of every description, rolled down earth collected from everywhere, onto the shield of Ajax, hoping to drive him off. But our illustrious leader, shaking his shield whenever it grew too heavy, relented not in the least. And Philoctetes, shooting from a distance, killed many of those on the wall and drove the others away.

In other parts of the field the rest of our soldiers met with equal success. That day would have seen the walls of Troy destroyed, the city sacked, if the swift arrival of night had not restrained us. Thus we returned to the ships, rejoicing, our spirits tremendously buoyed because of the deeds Philoctetes had done. To him we gave our highest praise and showed our deepest gratitude.

At daybreak, Philoctetes, accompanied by the rest of our leaders, returned to the field. And the Trojans, even with the help of their walls, could scarcely protect themselves, so great was their terror.

|21| Meanwhile Neoptolemus, now that his father's murder was avenged, began the mourning around Achilles' mound. Along with Phoenix and the entire army of the Myrmidons, he cut off his hair and placed it on the tomb. Thus they stayed there all the night.

During the same time, the sons of Antimachus (whom we have mentioned above) came to Helenus as representatives of Priam. But he refused to do as they begged, that is, to return to his people; and so they departed. Halfway back to the city, they were encountered by Diomedes and the other Ajax, and thus were captured and brought to the ships. When they had told who they were and explained their reason for coming, we, remembering how their father had spoken and plotted against our envoys,[8] ordered the soldiers to take them and lead them out where the Trojans could see and stone them to death.

At Troy, in a different direction, the relatives of Alexander, who were seeing to his burial, were carrying his body to Oenone. They say that Oenone—she had been married to him before his abduction of Helen—was so shocked by the sight of his body that she lost all power of speech, lost her spirit and, gradually being overwhelmed with grief, fell down dead. And thus a single tomb held her and him.

|22| All the Trojan nobles, since they saw the enemy raging more and more fiercely around their walls and knew that their

own resources were failing, felt that further resistance was hopeless. Accordingly, they plotted sedition against the princes and Priam. Having summoned Aeneas and the sons of Antenor, they were planning to return Helen to Menelaus, along with the things that had been carried off. But Deiphobus, having heard of their plans, took Helen off and married her himself.

When Priam entered the council, Aeneas heaped insults upon him. Finally the king yielded to the will of the nobles and ordered Antenor to go to the Greeks and seek an end to the war.

When Antenor signaled from the walls that the Trojans desired to negotiate, we granted permission. Thus he came to the ships, and we welcomed him gladly. Nestor, especially, told how faithful and kind he had been to the Greeks: his counsel and the aid of his sons had saved Menelaus from Trojan treachery. In return for what he had done, we promised to reward him richly when Troy was destroyed, and urged him to work with us— he knew we were friends—against those he knew to be treacherous.

Then, in a long speech, Antenor told how the gods were always punishing Trojan rulers for ill-considered acts. Laomedon, he said, had lied to Hercules—a famous story—and thus his kingdom had been destroyed. Then, through the influence of Hesione, Priam, who was still young and had had no share in all that had happened, had come to power; thereafter, becoming evil and foolish, he had been accustomed to attack everyone; he had killed and committed personal injuries, being sparing of his own property while seeking that of another. Such was the example which spread, like the worst of plagues, to his sons, who abstained from nothing either sacred or profane.

Antenor said that he himself was a very different person from Priam, in spite of the fact that they both were related to the Greeks by the same line of descent.[9] Hesione, the daughter of Danaus, was the mother of Electra, and Electra was the mother

of Dardanus; Dardanus had married Olizone, the daughter of
Phineus; their child was Erichthonius, who was the father of
Tros; and Tros was the father of Ilus, Ganymede, and Cleo-
mestra. Cleomestra was the mother of Assaracus, and Assaracus
had begotten Capys, the father of Anchises. Ilus had begotten
Tithonus and Laomedon, and Laomedon was the father of
Hicetaon, Clytius, Lampus, Thymoetes, Bucolion, and finally
Priam. As for himself, he was the son of Cleomestra and
Aesyetes. But Priam had disregarded every bond of kinship and
had acted with especial insolence and hatred toward his own
relations.

When he had finished this speech, he asked us to choose
representatives for the purpose of talking with him about peace;
as this was the reason the Trojan elders had sent him. Accordingly, we chose Agamemnon, Idomeneus, Ulysses, and Diomedes. Thereupon these plotted together, in secret, and decided,
among other things, that Aeneas, contingent upon his remaining
faithful, should share the spoils, nor should his house be harmed
in any way; as for Antenor, half of Priam's wealth should be given
to him; and one of his sons, whomever he chose, should rule over
Troy.

When they felt that their plans were complete, Antenor was
sent back to Troy to make a report far different from what they
had really decided. He was to say that the Greeks were preparing
an offering, a gift, for Minerva, and that, providing they recovered
Helen and received some gold, they were only too glad to abandon
the war and return to their people. Thus Antenor went off to Troy,
accompanied by Talthybius whose presence might help to produce
an illusion of trust.

Book Five

|1| When the arrival of Antenor and Talthybius was known at Troy, all the Trojans and their allies rushed to meet them, desiring to learn what had happened among the Greeks. But Antenor postponed his report until the next day, and so they dispersed and went home.

Then, at a banquet, in the presence of Talthybius, Antenor advised his sons to consider nothing so important in life as their long-standing friendship with Greece and recalled, with evident admiration, the honor, good faith, and guilelessness of individual Greeks.

After the meal, they parted company. But at daybreak Antenor and Talthybius went to the meeting of the council. (The elders were already there, eager to find some end to their dreadful afflictions.) Aeneas was the next to arrive, and then Priam and the rest of the princes. At last Antenor, having been ordered to tell what he had heard from the Greeks, spoke as follows:

|2| "It is a sad thing, Trojan princes and Trojan allies, it is a sad thing for us to be at war with the Greeks, but it is an even sadder and more painful thing that for the sake of a woman we have made enemies of the closest friends, of those who, being descendants of Pelops, are joined to us even by ties of marriage.

"If I may briefly touch on the past evils we have suffered, when has our city ever found rest, once it was lost in this quagmire of sorrows? When have we ever been without tears? When have you allies ever seen your misfortunes decrease? When have our friends, parents, relatives, and sons not been dying in battle? And, to sum up the rest of our sorrows with a personal allusion, what suffering have I not endured in the case of Glaucus, my son? His death, however, was not so painful to me as the fact that he had accompanied Alexander in the abduction of Helen.

"But enough of the past. Let us, at least, look to the future with caution and wisdom. The Greeks are faithful and true; they are rich in kindness and pious in doing their duty. Priam is a witness to this, for, in the very heat of the battle, he reaped the fruit of their pity. The Greeks were not so rash as to declare war against us until we had treated their envoys—even their envoys!—with treachery and guile. It is my opinion that Priam and his sons were to blame in this matter, and also Antimachus, who has recently paid for his guilt with the loss of his sons. But the real blame for everything that has happened rests upon Helen, that woman whom not even the Greeks really want to recover. Why should we keep this woman on whose account no nation, no people, has ever been friendly or even non-hostile to us? Shall we not, rather, eagerly beg the Greeks to take her again? And shall we not offer complete compensation for all the ways we have harmed them? Shall we not be reconciled with such men at least in the future?

"For my own part, I am leaving; I am going away. I refuse to share in these crimes any longer. There was a time when it was pleasing to live in this city; until now we had allies and friends; our relatives were safe, our country unharmed. But now we have partially or totally lost all of these things. Who can deny it? I can no longer endure to remain with those whose work is all destined to ruin along with the fall of their country.

"Until now, it is true, we have found some way to bury our dead; the enemy granted this favor. But now the altars and shrines of the gods have been criminally desecrated with human blood. And thus, being unable to hold our dear ones' funerals, we will suffer even more than when they died.

"At least prevent this from happening now. Our native land must be redeemed with gold and other ransom of this sort. There are many in our city who are rich; each must give whatever he can. We must offer the Greeks, in return for our lives, what they will have soon enough if they kill us. Let us give even the ornaments of our temples, if otherwise we cannot save our city.

"As for Priam, let only him keep all his wealth, let only him consider riches more important than his people, let him, the brooding miser, have even the things they carried off with Helen, and see how best to use his country's sorrows.

"Now our sins have found us out, and we are conquered."

|3| He was weeping as he spoke these and other things, and everyone was mourning. Stretching their hands toward heaven, they showed their agreement, praying, individually and together, that Priam, in view of their many adversities, should bring an end to their miseries. And finally, with one voice, they shouted that their native land must be redeemed.

Then Priam, tearing his hair and weeping in a pitiable way, addressed them. Now, he said, he was not only hated by the gods but was even considered a public enemy by his own people. Formerly he had had friends, relatives, and fellow citizens to comfort him in his misfortunes, but now none was to be found. He had wanted to begin negotiations when Alexander and Hector were living and not wait until now. No one, however, was able to remedy the past; they must plan for the present and put their hopes in the future. He offered all that he had for the redemption of Troy, and instructed Antenor to see to the matter. But now, since they hated him so, he was leaving their presence. Whatever they decided to do was agreeable to him.

|4| When the king had left, they decided that Antenor should return to the Greeks and learn what terms they wanted exactly; and that Aeneas, as he desired, should go along too. Thus the council broke up.

About midnight, Helen came to Antenor secretly. She sus-

pected that they were about to return her to Menelaus and feared
that she would be punished for having abandoned her home. Accordingly, she begged him to mention her, when he spoke among
the Greeks, and plead in her behalf. Now that Alexander was
dead, she hated all Troy, as they knew, and wanted to return to
her people.

At daybreak, Antenor and Aeneas came to the ships and
told us all about their city's decision. Then they withdrew with
those they had talked to before, to plan what action to take. It was
during these discussions about Troy and their nation that they
also told about Helen's desires and asked forgiveness for her;
and finally they agreed on how best to betray their city.

When they were ready, they returned to Troy, accompanied
by Ulysses and Diomedes. Ajax also wanted to go, but Aeneas
made him remain, arguing, no doubt, that the Trojans were afraid
of him no less than they had been afraid of Achilles and, therefore, might take him by treachery.

The hopes of all Trojans were raised when they saw that our
leaders had come. They thought this meant that war and conflict
were going to end. A meeting of the council was quickly called
and there, in the presence of our men, they decided, first of all, to
exile Antimachus from all of Phrygia, for he, to be sure, was the
cause of their terrible troubles. Then they began to discuss the
terms of peace.

|5| During their discussion, a huge crash and much shouting
suddenly arose from Pergamum, where Priam's palace was located. Those in the council, being thrown into confusion, ran outside and, thinking that the princes, as usual, had done some
treacherous deed, they rushed to the temple of Minerva. Soon
afterwards, however, they learned, from those who came from
the citadel, that the sons of Alexander, his children by Helen, had
perished, crushed when the roof of their home had collapsed. The
names of these sons were Bunomus,[1] Corythus, and Idaeus.

The business of the council was thus deferred, and our leaders went off to Antenor's, there to dine and spend the night. Moreover, they learned from Antenor about an oracle which once had informed the Trojans that Troy would fall in ruins, if the Palladium was carried outside the walls of the city. (The Palladium was an ancient statue in the temple of Minerva; it was made of wood, and had fallen from heaven and taken its place when Ilus was building the temple, and all but the roof was complete.)

Antenor agreed to help our men, just as they urged, in every way; he would do whatever they wanted. Nevertheless, he warned them that, at the meeting of the Trojan council, he would speak out boldly and openly oppose the demands the Greeks were making; in order, no doubt, to give the barbarians no grounds to suspect him.

Their plans being thus completed, at daybreak Antenor went, along with the Trojan nobles, to Priam; and our leaders returned to the ships.

|6| The sons of Alexander were buried with due ceremony. Three days later Idaeus came and summoned our leaders (those mentioned above). Panthus[2] and the other Trojans who were known for their wisdom made long speeches in which they explained that their previous actions had been rash and ill-advised. They had been constrained, they said, to act according to the will of the princes, by whom they were hated and counted as naught. They had not taken up arms against Greece willingly, for those who must follow another's command must look to his nod and try to obey it. Therefore, the Greeks should grant forgiveness and be willing to confer with those who had always been hoping for peace. Moreover, the Trojans had already suffered enough for their ill-advised acts.

After a long discussion of this point and that, finally the question of tribute was raised. Diomedes asked for five thousand talents of gold, and a like number of silver, besides one hundred thousand measures of wheat, for a period of ten years.

Then all the Trojans were silent, except for Antenor. He said that the Greeks were not acting like Greeks but barbarians. Since they demanded what was impossible, it was evident that they were planning for war under a pretext of peace. Moreover, Troy had never had as much gold and silver as Greece was demanding, not even before she had gone to the expense of hiring auxiliaries. If the Greeks persisted in these unscrupulous demands, the Trojans must shut their gates and burn the temples of their gods, and offer themselves and their country to one and the same destruction.

Diomedes answered: "We did not come from Argos to give special terms to Troy, but to fight you to the death. Therefore, if you are still desirous of war, the Greeks are ready, or if, as you say, you wish to burn your city, we will not prevent you. The Greeks, when treated unjustly, take vengeance. That is their way."

Then Panthus asked for a day's reprieve during which to ponder the Greek proposal. Thus our men went home with Antenor, and from there to the temple of Minerva.

|7| Meanwhile news of a remarkable portent was brought. It had occurred during the offering of sacrifices. Victims had been placed on the altars as usual. But the fire, having been lit, had not caught or burned in the usual way but had left the offerings untouched.

This news startled the people, and they rushed to the temple of Apollo to prove for themselves whether or not it was true. When they had placed parts of entrails on the altar and lit the fire, suddenly everything was thrown into confusion; the entrails fell to the ground. Then, while everyone was struck with astonishment, an eagle, swift and screeching, dove down and caught up a piece of the entrails and, soaring off, carried it away to the ships and there let it fall.

The Trojans received this omen as a great and very clear sign portending their doom. Diomedes and Ulysses, however, pretended not to know what had happened and walked around in the public square, like sightseers, marveling at the wonderful buildings of Troy.

We, at the ships, were also pondering the portent's meaning. And Calchas told us to be of good cheer, for we would be masters of Troy in short order.

|8| When Hecuba learned of the portent, she went to placate the gods, especially Minerva and Apollo, with many gifts and rich sacrifices. But just as before, the fire refused to burn the victims and died out quickly.

Then Cassandra became divinely inspired and ordered the victims to be carried to Hector's tomb. She said that the gods were angry and were rejecting their sacrifices because of the crime they had recently committed against the religion of Apollo. Thus, following her orders, they slew the bulls and took them to Hector's pyre, where, when the fire was lit, the sacrifice was completely consumed. With the coming of evening, they returned to their homes.

During that night Antenor secretly went to the temple of Minerva and, threatening the priestess Theano[3] with force and promising that she would be richly rewarded, begged her to give the Palladium to him. This she did; and thus he, being true to our men, carried it off to them. And they, having wrapped it up so that no one could tell what it was, sent it away in a cart to the hut of Ulysses through close and faithful friends.

With the coming of dawn, the Trojan council met. When our envoys had entered, Antenor, as though fearing the wrath of the Greeks, begged their forgiveness for having previously spoken so boldly against them in behalf of his native land.

Ulysses replied that he was not disturbed by this so much as by the fact that negotiations were being prolonged, especially when the favorable time for sailing was quickly passing.

After a long discussion, they finally agreed on a sum of two thousand talents of gold and two thousand of silver.

Then our envoys returned to the ships to make their report to our men. When our leaders had been assembled, they told them all that had been said and done, and how Antenor had carried the

Palladium off. Thereupon, since all our leaders thought best, the rest of the soldiers were given the news.

|9| In view of these developments we decided unanimously to show our gratitude to Minerva by making a splendid offering to her. Helenus was summoned to tell us how to proceed. Using his prophetic powers (he had not been informed), he was able to give a detailed account of everything that had happened so far. And he also said that Troy was doomed now that the Palladium, the safeguard of Troy, had been carried away. We must, he said, offer a wooden horse to Minerva; this gift would prove fatal to Troy. The horse must be so large that the Trojans would have to breach their walls; Antenor would urge and advise them to do this. As Helenus was speaking, the thought of his father, Priam, and of his brothers who were still living caused him to burst into tears; his grief was so strong that he lost all control of himself and collapsed.

When he had come to his senses and was able to rise, Neoptolemus took him in charge. He had him guarded for fear he might somehow inform the enemy about what had happened. But Helenus, seeing himself under guard, told Neoptolemus there was nothing to worry about, for he would prove faithful and, after Troy's fall, would live with Neoptolemus in Greece many years.

And so, following Helenus' advice, we brought in a great deal of wood for building the horse. Epeus and Ajax the son of Oileus were in charge of this work.

|10| Meanwhile ten leaders were chosen to go to Troy and ratify the terms of the peace: Diomedes, Ulysses, Idomeneus, Ajax the son of Telamon, Nestor, Meriones, Thoas, Philoctetes, Neoptolemus, and Eumelus.

The Trojans, seeing our men in their public square, rejoiced, believing that now their afflictions would end. Individually and in groups, whenever they met them, they greeted them warmly and embraced them like loved ones.

Priam implored our leaders on behalf of Helenus and com-mended him to them with many prayers. Helenus, he said, was his dearest son, dearer because of his wisdom than all of the others.

When dinnertime came, the Trojans held a public banquet in honor of the Greeks and in celebration of the peace they were making. Antenor was host and graciously served every need of our men.

At daybreak all the elders convened in the temple of Minerva, and Antenor officially announced that ten envoys had been sent by the Greeks to ratify the terms of the peace. There-upon the envoys were escorted into the council, and they and the elders shook hands. It was decided to ratify the peace on the fol-lowing day. Sacred oaths must be sworn, for the purpose of which altars must be raised in the center of the plain where all could see.

When preparations had been made, Diomedes and Ulysses were first to swear. Calling on Highest Jupiter, Mother Earth, Sun, Moon, and Ocean to be their witnesses, they promised to abide by the agreements which they had made with Antenor. Then they walked through the center of the portions of the sacrificial victims. (Two victims had been brought, the portions of which had been laid out, half in an easterly direction and half in the direction of our ships.) Diomedes and Ulysses were followed by Antenor, who took the same oath. After ratifying the terms of the peace in this way, both sides returned to their people.

The barbarians heaped highest praises upon Antenor, rever-encing him like a god whenever he approached. They believed that he alone was responsible for the treaty and peace with the Greeks.

Now everywhere, as both sides wished, war had ceased. Greeks felt free to go to Troy. Trojans came among the ships. And the Trojan allies—those who were still alive—went home, taking advantage of the treaty and feeling thankful for peace, not even waiting to be paid for their hardships and troubles, fearing, no doubt, that the barbarians would somehow break the agreements. |11| During this time, at the ships, Epeus, following Helenus' advice, was directing the building of the wooden horse. It towered to an immense height. Wheels were put beneath its feet to make it easier to draw along. It was the greatest offering ever to be given to Minerva. Everyone said so.

At Troy, Antenor and Aeneas were making sure that the exact amount of gold and silver, in accordance with the terms of the peace, was carried to the temple of Minerva.

And we, having learned that the allies of the Trojans had left, were careful to keep the terms of the peace. There was no more killing and no more wounding, lest the barbarians suspect that we were breaking agreements.

When the wooden horse had been built, complete in all points, we drew it out to the walls. The Trojans were told to receive it religiously as a sacred offering to Minerva. They poured from their gates and joyously welcomed the horse. A sacrifice was made, and they drew it nearer the city. When, however, they saw that the horse was too large to pass through their gates, they decided, their enthusiasm blinding them to any objections, to tear down their walls. Thus they all joined in, and tore down their walls, those walls which had stood for centuries unharmed, and which, as tradition told, were the masterwork of Neptune and Apollo.[4]

When the work of demolition was almost complete, the Greeks purposely caused a delay. We said that the Trojans must pay the gold and silver they had promised before they could draw the horse into Troy. Thus there was an interval of time during which, the walls being half demolished, Ulysses hired all of the Trojan carpenters to help repair the ships.

When our fleet had thus been put in order, along with all of our sailing gear, and when the gold and silver had been paid, we ordered the Trojans to continue their work of destruction. As soon as a part of the walls was down, a crowd of joking men and women merrily hastened to draw the horse within their city.

|12| Meanwhile we, having stowed everything on the ships and having set fire to our huts, sailed off to Sigeum and there awaited the night.

When the Trojans, being worn out with carousing and feeling happy and secure because of the peace, had fallen asleep, we returned to the city, sailing through the dead silence, following the beacon that Sinon raised from his hidden position. Soon we had entered the walls and divided the city among us. At a given signal, we slaughtered whomever we found—in homes, on streets, in places sacred and profane. Some of the Trojans awoke, but these were cut down before they could reach for their arms or think of a way to escape. There was, in short, no end to death and slaughter. Parents and children were killed, while loved ones watched and lamented, and then the latter were killed—a pitiable sight. With equal dispatch, the buildings of the city were set on fire and destroyed; the only homes to be saved were those of Aeneas and Antenor, where guards had been posted. Priam, seeing what was happening, fled to the altar of Jupiter that stood in front of the palace. And many members of the royal family fled to other shrines of the gods; Cassandra, for instance, went to the temple of Minerva. All who fell into the hands of the enemy died cruelly, without anyone to avenge them.

At daybreak our forces came to the house where Helen was living with Deiphobus. He (as already described) had taken her to wife when Alexander had died. Now Menelaus tortured him to death, brutally cutting him to pieces, lopping off ears and arms and nose and so forth.

And Neoptolemus, with no respect for old age or the office of king, slaughtered Priam, both of whose hands were clutching the altar.

And Ajax the son of Oileus dragged off Cassandra from the temple of Minerva to be his captive.

|13| Thus we destroyed Troy and the Trojans. But still there were those who were seeking protection at the altars of gods. We decided unanimously to pull them away and kill them; so great was our lust for vengeance and our will to destroy the power of the Trojans. Accordingly, those who had escaped the slaughter of the previous night, those trembling sheep, were slaughtered. And, as is usual in war, we pillaged the temples and half-burned houses, and for many a day hunted down any of the enemy who might have escaped. Places were designated where objects of gold and of silver and costly garments were brought.

When we were sated with Trojan blood, and the city was burned to the ground, we divided the booty, in payment of our military service, beginning with the captive women and children. First of all, Helen was freely given to Menelaus; then Polyxena, at the request of Ulysses, was given to Neoptolemus, to sacrifice to Achilles; Cassandra was given to Agamemnon (he had been so moved by her beauty that, in spite of himself, he had openly said that he loved her); and Aethra and Clymene were given to Demophoon and Acamas. The other women were apportioned by lot, and thus Andromache fell to Neoptolemus (to honor whose greatness, we further allowed Andromache's sons to accompany her); and Hecuba fell to Ulysses. After enslaving the women of royal birth, we allotted booty and captives to the rest of our men in proportion as they deserved.

|14| Heated contention arose at this time as to which of our leaders should have the Palladium.[5] Ajax the son of Telamon demanded it in payment for the booty his courage and zeal had brought to us all. There was almost no one who was willing to offend a man of such greatness, for we vividly remembered his deeds on offense and defense. Only Diomedes and Ulysses stood in his way; they based their claims to the Palladium on the fact

that they had carried it off. But Ajax swore that Antenor, who had hoped thereby to win their friendship, had carried the Palladium off; and this, he said, had caused them no trouble and made no demands on their courage. Thereupon Diomedes modestly yielded to Ajax. But not so Ulysses, who contended, with all of his force, that he should have the Palladium.

Menelaus and Agamemnon favored the cause of Ulysses, for they remembered how Helen had been saved, just a little before, by his aid. When Troy had been taken, Ajax had been the first to propose that she should be killed because of the troubles and sufferings she had caused for so long a time. Many good men had assented. But Menelaus, still loving his wife, had gone the rounds, and plead for her life, and finally, through the intercession of Ulysses, had won her back unharmed.

And so we decided between Ajax and Ulysses, judging only their merits in this particular case. It made no difference which was the bravest. Yes, Ajax had performed many valorous deeds, and brought back grain from Thrace, but these were matters not pertinent here. Thus, in spite of the fact that we were surrounded by enemies and still threatened with war, the Palladium went to Ulysses.

|15| This decision caused our men to split into two factions: those who, remembering the brave deeds of Ajax, thought that no one was better than he; and those who favored Ulysses. Ajax was so angry that he lost control of himself and openly swore to kill those who had thwarted his claim. Accordingly, Ulysses, Agamemnon, and Menelaus increased their guard and kept careful watch for their personal safety. With the coming of night, as we departed, we all cursed and reviled the two kings, blaming them for letting the lust for a woman endanger the army.

At daybreak we found Ajax, out in the open, dead; upon closer investigation, we discovered that he had been killed with a sword. A great tumult arose among our leaders and men, and soon a full-grown rebellion was under way. We felt that just as Palamedes, our wisest counselor in war and peace, had been treacherously slain, so now Ajax, our most distinguished commander, had met a similar end.

Agamemnon and Menelaus stayed in their huts, guarded by trusted companions, and avoided any possible violence.

Meanwhile Neoptolemus brought wood and cremated the body of Ajax; then he gathered the remains in a golden urn and had them buried in Rhoeteum.[6] He also dedicated a monument in honor of Ajax, and this was quickly constructed.

If Ajax had died before Troy had been taken, certainly the cause of the enemy would have been greatly promoted. Who knows how the war might have ended?

Ulysses, knowing that he was hated by the army, feared personal violence, and fled across to Ismaros. He left the Palladium behind for Diomedes to have.

|16| After the departure of Ulysses, Hecuba, preferring death to enslavement, called down many curses and evil omens upon us, and we, being terribly provoked, stoned her to death. Her tomb, which was raised at Abydos, was called Cynossema (The Tomb of the Bitch) because of her mad and shameless barking.

At the same time Cassandra, inspired by the god, predicted that Agamemnon would die, treacherously slaughtered by members of his household. Furthermore, she said, death and disaster awaited the rest of the Greeks, as they tried to return to their homelands.

Antenor begged us, in behalf of his people, to forget about vengeance and think of ourselves, for the time for sailing was passing. Having invited our leaders to dinner, he loaded them down with marvelous gifts.

Our leaders were urging Aeneas to sail along with us to Greece and promised to give him a kingdom as powerful as any they ruled.

Helenus was rewarded with the sons of Hector, whom Neoptolemus gave him, and with all the gold and silver which the rest of our leaders felt they should give him.

Then a meeting of the council was called, and we decided to hold a public funeral, to last for three days, in honor of Ajax. When the third day came to an end, all of our kings cut off their hair, which then they placed on the tomb.

From this time on, we began to revile Agamemnon and Menelaus, saying that they were not the sons of Atreus but of Plisthenes, and therefore ignoble. They, hoping that if they were gone our hatred would vanish, begged us to let them depart without harm. This we permitted; and so, like outcasts or exiles, they were the first to set sail.

We gave the sons of Ajax to Teucer. They were Aeantides and Eurysaces, whose mothers were Glauce and Tecmessa respectively.

|17| Winter was coming on fast and threatened to prevent us from sailing. Accordingly, we drew our ships down to the sea and fitted them out with oars and other equipment. Then we departed, each with the booty he had gained for all those years of fighting.

After our departure, Aeneas, who had been left behind at Troy, tried to drive Antenor out of the kingdom. Leaving the city, he approached all those who were inhabitants of Dardanum and the peninsula nearby, and begged them to help him. He was unsuccessful, however; and when he tried to return to Troy, Antenor, who had learned what was happening, refused him admittance. And so Aeneas was forced to set sail. Taking all of his patrimony, he departed from Troy and eventually arrived in the Adriatic Sea, after passing many barbarous peoples. Here he and those who were with him founded a city, which they called Corcyra Melaena (Black Corcyra).

When it was known at Troy that Antenor had gained control of the kingdom, all the survivors of the war, those who had escaped the slaughter of that fearful night, supported his rule. In practically no time his following had increased to immense proportions. Everyone loved him and trusted his wisdom. His closest friend was Oenideus, the king of the Cebrenians.

I, Dictys of Cnossos, the companion of Idomeneus, have written this account in the language (how many there are!) I best understand, using the Phoenician alphabet bequeathed to us by Cadmus and Danaus. No one should marvel that many different languages are spoken on this one island of mine, for such is the case all over Greece. Everything I have written about the war between the Greeks and the barbarians, in which I took a very active part, is based on first-hand knowledge. What I have told about Antenor and his kingdom was learned on inquiry from others.

Now it is time to relate the returns of our men.

Book Six

|1| When the Greeks had loaded the ships with all the booty they had gained, and gone aboard themselves, they weighed anchor and set sail. Blessed with a favorable wind from the stern quarter, within a few days they reached the Aegean Sea. But then, as fate would have it, a furious storm arose, a sea of troubles for all of our men, and scattered our ships.

Shattering lightning bolts, which terrified the sailors and caused them to lose all control, completely destroyed the fleet of the Locrians, commanded by Ajax. Ajax and some of the others who, having escaped the wreckage, kept afloat by clinging to boards and flotsam, were dashed to death against the Choeradian crags of Euboea. The night had kept them from seeing; and Nauplius, knowing their plight and desiring to avenge the death of his son Palamedes, had raised a torch, to lure them there, as if to a harbor.

|2| At the same time Oeax, who was the son of Nauplius and the brother of Palamedes, on learning that the Greeks were returning home, went to Argos and reported, falsely, to Clytemnestra and Aegiale that Agamemnon and Diomedes were bringing back women they preferred to their wives; and he added those things by which their womanly hearts, by nature easily persuaded, might be the more incensed against their husbands. Thus they were prompted to arm themselves against their husbands' arrivals. Accordingly, Aegiale, with the help of the citizens, prevented Diomedes from entering the city; and Clytemnestra had Aegisthus,

with whom she was living in adultery, snare Agamemnon and slay him. Soon thereafter the adulterous pair were married, and Clytemnestra gave birth to a daughter, Erigone.

Meanwhile Talthybius saved Orestes, Agamemnon's son, from the hands of Aegisthus, and turned him over to Idomeneus.

Idomeneus was then a resident of Corinth; to which city Diomedes and Teucer also came when driven away from their homes. Teucer had been prohibited from landing on Salamis by Telamon, his father, because, no doubt, he had not prevented his brother Ajax' ignominious death.

Meanwhile the Athenians welcomed Menestheus along with Aethra, the daughter of Pittheus, and her daughter, Clymene. Demophoon and Acamas, however, remained outside the city.

Most of those who had escaped death from dangers at sea or plots at home came to Corinth and there made plans to recover their kingdoms. They should, they thought, combine their forces and attack their kingdoms one at a time. This action, however, was vetoed by Nestor, who said that they should try persuasion first and not tear Greece apart with civil wars.

Soon after this, Diomedes learned that his grandfather, Oeneus, was being afflicted in every way by those who had gained control of Aetolia during his absence. Accordingly, he went to that region and killed the guilty usurpers. Those who favored his cause easily welcomed him back, for all Aetolia feared him.

When news of Diomedes' success spread, all of the Greeks reinstated their kings, thinking that no one could match the bravery or strength of those who had battled at Troy. And so we Cretans and our king Idomeneus returned to our native soil and were joyfully received by our people.

|3| When Orestes had grown to maturity, he begged Idomeneus to give him as many men as he could and let him sail from Crete to Athens. His request being granted, having gathered a number

of those he thought sufficient, he went off to Athens and there invoked the aid of the Athenians against Aegisthus.

Then, having gone to the oracle, he received the response that he was destined to kill his mother and Aegisthus, and thus to recover his father's kingdom.

Armed with this prophecy, he and his band went on to Strophius, the Phocian. Strophius willingly offered his aid, for he passionately hated Aegisthus. (Aegisthus had first married Strophius' daughter, but then had rejected her and married Clytemnestra; and he had treacherously slain Agamemnon, the great king.)

Thus Orestes, having assembled a large army, marched on Mycenae. Clytemnestra was immediately slain, along with many others who dared to resist. Aegisthus was absent. But when news of his arrival was brought, he was ambushed and killed. Throughout Argos the people were forced to take sides and tried to choose where best their interest lay.

During the same time Menelaus landed on Crete and learned how Agamemnon had died and what was happening in Argos.

|4| When the Cretans heard of Helen's arrival, many men and women from all over the island came together, desiring to see her for whose sake almost all of the world had gone to war.

Menelaus told his adventures. He had learned that Teucer, who had been banished from home, had founded a city on Cyprus called Salamis. He also reported the many wonders of Egypt. The serpents there, he said, had killed his pilot, Canopus; for whom he had built a magnificent tomb.

When the time seemed right, Menelaus sailed to Mycenae. There he laid many plots against Orestes, but the people prevented him from carrying out these plans. Orestes, it was decided unanimously, should go to Athens and there stand trial before the court of Areopagus. Thus Orestes plead his case, and the Areopagus acquitted him; this court was reputedly the most severe in all Greece.

This acquittal so grieved Orestes' half-sister, Erigone, who was the daughter of Aegisthus, that she hanged herself. After the verdict and after Orestes had been purified by every means, according to the ancient ritual in use for parricides, Menestheus sent him home to Mycenae.

And thereupon the people made him king.

Later Orestes and then Menelaus came to Crete at the invitation of Idomeneus. Orestes bitterly charged his uncle with plotting against him at a time when his position was already endangered by public strife. Finally, however, they were reconciled with each other by the intercession of Idomeneus and so departed to Lacedaemon. And then Menelaus, just as he had agreed to do, promised Hermione in marriage to Orestes.

|5| During the same time Ulysses, with two ships he had hired from the Phoenicians, landed on Crete.[1] He had lost his fleet along with his comrades and all of his booty and had barely escaped with his life by using his wits. This disaster had been due to the power of Telamon, who no doubt hated Ulysses for being the cause of Ajax' death.

When Idomeneus asked Ulysses how he had met such misfortunes, he told the story of his wanderings from the beginning. First they had landed at Ismaros, where they had fought, and gained much booty.

Then they had sailed to the country of the Lotus-Eaters, where they had met with a cruel fate.

Then they had gone to the island of Sicily, where the brothers Cyclops and Laestrygon had treated them with every indignity and where Polyphemus and Antiphates, who were the sons of the former, had killed many of them. Finally, however, Polyphemus —he was the king—had taken pity upon them and agreed to a truce. But then they had tried to carry off Polyphemus' daughter Arene, who had fallen desperately in love with their comrade Alphenor. Polyphemus, however, had discovered their plans.

Thus, having been forcibly deprived of the girl, they were driven away—out through the islands of Aeolus, on to the island of Circe, and then to the island of Calypso. It was well known how these queens, by using certain charms, enticed their guests to love them. Nevertheless, Ulysses escaped.

Then they had gone to that place where, having performed the requisite rites, they learned of the future from the shades of the dead.

Then on past the rocks of the Sirens, whom he had cleverly eluded.

And then, finally, he had lost most of his ships and men to Scylla and Charybdis, that savage, whirling pool that sucks down everything within its reach.

Then he and the survivors had come into the hands of Phoenician pirates, and these had mercifully saved them.

Thereupon our king Idomeneus did as Ulysses wished and gave him two ships and much booty and sent him off to Alcinous, the king of the Phaeacians.

|6| There they already knew of his fame and entertained him many days. Also they told him that Penelope was being wooed by thirty handsome suitors who had come from different regions —from Zacynthus, the Echinades, Leucas, and Ithaca. Thereupon he prevailed upon Alcinous to sail with him, to avenge this insult to his marriage.

When they had come to Ithaca, Ulysses stayed concealed for a little while, until they could inform Telemachus of what they were planning. Then they proceeded to the palace and slew the suitors, who had been wined and dined to the full. When the people knew that Ulysses had come, they welcomed him back and showed that they favored his cause; and from them he learned everything that had happened at home. Ulysses repaid the faithful with gifts, the unfaithful with punishments. As for Penelope, her reputation for virtue is famous.

Soon afterwards, in answer to Ulysses' hopes and prayers, Nausicaa, the daughter of Alcinous, was married to Telemachus. This was also the time when our leader Idomeneus died in Crete; and, according to the right of succession, the kingdom passed to Meriones. Laertes, three years after his son had returned, ended his life. Nausicaa and Telemachus had a son, to whom Ulysses gave the name Ptoliporthus (Sacker of Cities).

|7| While these things were happening on Ithaca, Neoptolemus was among the Molossians repairing his ships, which had been wrecked in a storm. There he had learned that Acastus had driven Peleus out of his kingdom in Thessaly. Accordingly, as he desired to avenge this wrong to his grandfather, he sent Chrysippus and Aratus to explore the situation; they were very reliable men, and no one in Thessaly knew them.

These learned from Assandrus, a follower of Peleus, everything that had happened and how Acastus had treacherously attacked Peleus. This Assandrus had eluded the tyranny of Acastus and sided with Peleus, with whom he had become so intimate that he was able to tell, among other things, about Peleus' marriage with Thetis, Chiron's daughter.

At that time many kings had been invited from everywhere to the wedding, which was at Chiron's home. During the banquet they had praised the bride and offered her toasts as if to a goddess, saying that she was a Nereid and that Chiron was Nereus. In the same way they had called any of their number who excelled in dancing or singing Apollo or Bacchus, and had given the names of Muses to many of the women. Accordingly, from that time on, this banquet was known as "a banquet of the gods."

|8| When Chrysippus and Aratus had learned what they wanted to know, they returned to Neoptolemus and made a full report.

Thereupon Neoptolemus, though the sea was rough and there were reasons enough to stay where he was, equipped his fleet and set sail. Having been much harassed on sea by a savage storm and having been driven to the shore of the Sepiades (so called because of their dangerous rocks), he lost almost all of his ships; he himself and those who were sailing with him barely escaped. There he found his grandfather, Peleus, who was hiding in a dark, secluded cave. The old man, while avoiding the treacherous plots of Acastus, was keeping a lookout for all who happened to sail there, hoping his grandson would come.

When Peleus had told Neoptolemus all that had befallen his house, the latter was beginning to decide on a plan of attack when by chance he learned that the sons of Acastus, Menalippus and Plisthenes, were coming to hunt near Peleus' cave. Accordingly, he changed into the clothes of that region; and then, pretending to be an Iolchian, he presented himself to the sons of Acastus and asked permission to join in their sport. This being granted, soon afterwards he came upon Menalippus and Plisthenes—they were close together but separated some distance from the rest of their party—and slew them. Then he captured and slew their faithful slave, Cinyras, who had come in search of his masters; but not before he had learned that Acastus also was coming.

|9| Thereupon Neoptolemus changed into Phrygian clothes, so as to look like Mestor, the son of Priam, whom he had brought along as a captive.[2] When, dressed in this guise, he met with Acastus, he claimed to be Mestor and said that Neoptolemus was wearied from sailing and was sleeping there in the cave.

Since Acastus desired to trap this most hated of enemies, he went straight to the cave. But Thetis was there and kept him from entering. (She, having learned what was happening, had come to be with Peleus.) She roundly berated Acastus for his crimes against the house of Achilles and against the laws of the gods.

But then she used her influence to save him from Neoptolemus' power, for she urged her grandson to refrain from further vengeance and slaughter.

Acastus, being grateful for his unexpected escape, willingly, right then and there, gave Neoptolemus complete control of the kingdom.

Then Neoptolemus, having gained control of the kingdom, went to the city with his grandfather, Peleus, and his grandmother, Thetis, and those of his men who had survived the voyage. All the citizens and all the people round about who were under his power welcomed him joyously and with a devotion which, as he was soon to prove, was not misplaced.

|10| Neoptolemus told me everything which I have written about him, when I attended his marriage to Hermione, the daughter of Menelaus. I also learned from him about the burial of Memnon's remains.

Memnon's bones came into the hands of those of his men who had stayed on Paphos. They had slain Pallas,[3] under whose leadership they were sailing to Troy, and had taken the booty for themselves.

Then his sister Himera, or Hemera as some call her after her mother,[4] came to Paphos, looking for the body of her brother. When she found the remains and learned what had happened to the booty, she wanted to recover both. Thereupon, through the influence of the Phoenicians, who composed a majority of Memnon's soldiers there, she was given a choice: she could have either the booty or the bones, but not both. Accordingly, yielding to sisterly affection, she chose the latter; she took the urn and, setting sail, carried it off to Phoenicia.

When she had come to the part of this country called Phalliotis, she buried the urn. Then she suddenly vanished from sight. There were three explanations for her disappearance: either she had vanished at sunset along with her mother, Himera; or she had killed herself, overwhelmed with grieving over her brother; or the inhabitants of Phalliotis had killed her, desiring to steal whatever she had.

Neoptolemus is my source for what I have told about Memnon and his sister.

|11| The year after I returned to Crete, I went to the oracle of Apollo as a public representative, along with two others, in order to seek relief from a plague. For no apparent reason and all unexpectedly, a great horde of locusts had attacked our island and was destroying all of the crops in the fields. The response of the oracle, in answer to our many prayers and supplications, was that living creatures must die, divinely slain, before the crops of our island would grow and abound.

The people at Delphi prohibited us from sailing home at this time; the weather, they said, was unfavorable and dangerous. Nevertheless, Lycophron and Ixaeus—they were the two who had come along with me—refused to obey this injunction. Thus they sailed. When, however, they were half way to Crete, a bolt of lightning struck them dead. And then, just as the god had predicted, with the same bolt of lightning, the locusts departed, swallowed up by the sea, and the crops of our island began to increase.

|12| During the same time Neoptolemus, having consummated his marriage with Hermione, went to Delphi. He wanted to give thanks to Apollo for the fact that Alexander, who had murdered his father, had paid for his crime. Andromache was left behind at home, along with Laodamas, her only surviving son by Hector.[5]

Now Hermione, after the departure of her husband, was tortured by the thought of her captive rival, and summoned her father, Menelaus. Then, bitterly complaining about her poor treatment—how Neoptolemus preferred a captive woman to her —she urged Menelaus to kill Hector's son. Andromache, however, having learned of this plot, saved her son and escaped with the aid of the people, who pitied her fate; furthermore, these heaped abuses upon Menelaus, and were barely prevented from killing him.

|13| Meanwhile Orestes arrived and learned all that was happening. Thereupon he urged Menelaus to carry out the plot, for he himself was planning to kill Neoptolemus when he returned. He hated Neoptolemus for having married Hermione; she had been promised to him. Accordingly, the first thing he did was to send some trusted scouts to Delphi to find out when Neoptolemus would come.

Menelaus, being thus apprised of Orestes' plans, returned to Sparta, for he wanted no part in such a crime.

Then the scouts who had been sent to Delphi reported that Neoptolemus was not to be found in that place. And thus Orestes was forced to set out in search of his man.

When he returned—but not on the same day he had left— everyone believed that he had accomplished his purpose. Within a short time the popular story was that Neoptolemus was dead and that Orestes had treacherously slain him.

Then Orestes returned to Mycenae, taking Hermione with him. She had been promised to him.

Meanwhile Peleus and Thetis, having heard of their grandson's death, set out to learn for themselves exactly how he had died. They discovered that he had been buried at Delphi (where then they performed his funeral rites according to custom), but that he had died in a place where Orestes had never been seen. This, however, the people refused to believe, so strong was their presumption of Orestes' treachery.

Furthermore, Thetis, seeing that Hermione and Orestes were married, sent Andromache off to the Molossians. Andromache was pregnant by Neoptolemus, and Thetis feared that Orestes and Hermione might try to kill the baby.

|14| During the same time Ulysses had been frightened by fre-

quent omens and nightmares. Accordingly, he summoned all those in his area who were skilled in interpreting dreams, and told them everything, but especially this dream he frequently had:[6]

A form, half human and half divine,[7] and beautiful to behold, suddenly arose from the same place. As he passionately reached out his arms and tried to embrace it, he received a rebuke, in a human voice: such a union was wicked, a union between those of the same flesh and blood, one of whom was destined to die at the hands of the other. And while he pondered and wondered how this could be, a shaft, hurled by the apparition's command, appeared to arise from the sea and, coming between them, caused them to part.

Everyone who was there interpreted this vision as fatal to him; and, furthermore, they begged him to beware of the treacherous acts of his son. Accordingly, Telemachus, because of his father's suspicions, was sent to the island of Cephalenia, there to farm where trusted guards could watch him. Furthermore, Ulysses, by withdrawing into a region that was hidden and remote, strove to avoid what his dream had foretold.

|15| Meanwhile, however, Telegonus, whom Circe had borne to Ulysses and raised on the island of Aeaea, having grown to manhood, came to Ithaca in search of his father. He was carrying a spear, whose point was the bone of a sea bird, the turtle-dove, which was the symbol of Aeaea, where he was born. When he learned where Ulysses was living off in the country, he went to that place; but the guards there prohibited him entry. Persisting but always being resisted, he began to shout that this was disgraceful, a crime, to prevent a son from embracing his father. But the guards, not knowing that Ulysses had fathered a second son and believing that this was Telemachus who had come to murder the king, resisted ever more fiercely. And thus Telegonus, becoming more and more angry because of this increasingly vehement opposition, ended by killing or wounding many of the guards.

Ulysses, having learned what was happening, thought that this was a young man whom Telemachus had sent to harm him. Accordingly, he entered the fray and let fly with his spear, which he always carried for protection. Telegonus, however, parried the blow; and then, aiming to make a mortal wound and letting fly with his own remarkable weapon, he hit his father.

Ulysses, as he fell, was thankful for this sort of fate. It was all for the best, he thought; by dying at the hands of a foreigner he would prevent Telemachus, whom he dearly loved, from being guilty of parricide. Still breathing, he asked the young man who he was and where he was from and how he had dared to kill Ulysses, the son of Laertes, a man famous for virtues in war and peace.

And then Telegonus realized that this was his father whom he had slain. He wept in a very pitiable way and pulled his hair with both his hands, being terribly tortured because he had caused his father's death. Then, as Ulysses had asked, he told him his name and the name of his mother and the name of the island where he was born; and he showed him the point of the spear.

And so Ulysses knew that his recurring dream had been correctly interpreted; he had been fatally struck by one whom he had never suspected. And thus, within three days, he died, a man advanced in years, whose strength, however, was as yet unimpaired.

THE
FALL OF TROY
A HISTORY
by
Dares the Phrygian

[Letter]¹

Cornelius Nepos sends greetings to his Sallustius Crispus.

While I was busily engaged in study at Athens, I found the history which Dares the Phrygian wrote about the Greeks and the Trojans. As its title indicates, this history was written in Dares' own hand. I was very delighted to obtain it and immediately made an exact translation into Latin, neither adding nor omitting anything, nor giving any personal touch. Following the straightforward and simple style of the Greek original, I translated word for word.

Thus my readers can know exactly what happened according to this account and judge for themselves whether Dares the Phrygian or Homer wrote the more truthfully—Dares, who lived and fought at the time the Greeks stormed Troy, or Homer, who was born long after the War was over. When the Athenians judged this matter, they found Homer insane for describing gods battling with mortals. But so much for this. Let us now turn to what I have promised.   •   •   •

|1| King Pelias, who ruled in the Peloponnese,¹ was the brother of Aeson, and Aeson was the father of Jason.

Jason was known for his courage and goodness. He treated everyone in the realm as his personal friend, and therefore everyone loved him.

When King Pelias saw that Jason was popular with everyone, he feared that he might do him some harm or drive him out of the kingdom. Accordingly, he told Jason that there was something worthy of his prowess at Colchis: the golden fleece of a ram. If Jason would bring it back, he would give him complete control of the kingdom.

On hearing this, Jason, who was the bravest of men, since he desired to see the world and hoped to add to his glory by bringing the golden fleece from Colchis, told the king he wanted to go. He needed, however, supplies and companions.

King Pelias ordered the architect-craftsman Argus to come and build the most beautiful ship he could, according to Jason's specifications. Thus the rumor went throughout Greece that they were building a ship and that Jason was going to Colchis to fetch the golden fleece. Friends and acquaintances came and promised to go along with him. Jason was grateful to them and urged them to prepare to sail. When the ship was finished and the time for sailing had come, he sent them notice by letter. Immediately those who had promised to go along with him assembled at the ship, to which the name Argo was given.

King Pelias, after ordering the necessary supplies to be stowed, exhorted Jason and those who were about to set forth with him to show their courage. They must, he said, accomplish their mission, for this was a voyage which surely would glorify Greece and themselves.

(It is not our business to tell about those who set forth with Jason. If anyone wishes to know about them, he should read the *Argonautica*.[2])

|2| When Jason came to Phrygia, he docked at the port of the Simois River, and everyone went ashore.

Soon news was brought to King Laomedon that a strange ship unexpectedly had entered the port of the Simois, and that many young men had come in it from Greece. On hearing this, the king was disturbed. Thinking that it would endanger the public welfare if Greeks began landing on his shores, he sent word to the port for the Greeks to depart from his boundaries. If they refused to obey, he would drive them out forcibly.

Jason and those who had come with him were deeply upset at the barbarous way Laomedon was treating them; they had done him no harm. Nevertheless, they were afraid to oppose him. They were not ready for battle and would certainly be crushed by the greater forces of the barbarians.

Thus, reembarking, they departed from Phrygia.

And set out for Colchis.

And stole the fleece.

And returned to their homeland.

|3| Hercules was deeply upset at the insulting way Laomedon had treated him and those who had gone with Jason to Colchis. He went to Sparta and urged Castor and Pollux to help him take vengeance against Laomedon, saying that if only they promised their aid, many others would follow. Castor and Pollux promised to do whatever he wanted.

He departed from them and went on to Salamis. There he visited Telamon and asked him to join the expedition against Troy, to avenge the ill-treatment he and his people had suffered. Telamon promised that he was ready for anything Hercules wanted to do.

He set out from Salamis and went on to Phthia. There he asked Peleus to join the expedition against Troy. Peleus promised to go.

Next he went to Pylos to visit Nestor. When Nestor asked why he had come, Hercules answered that he was stirred to seek vengeance and that he was leading an army against Phrygia. Nestor praised him and promised his aid.

Hercules, knowing that he had everyone's support, readied his ships and gathered an army. When the time for sailing was right, he sent letters to those he had asked and told them to come in full force. On their arrival, they all set sail for Phrygia.

They came to Sigeum at night. Hercules, Telamon, and Peleus led the army into the country, leaving Castor, Pollux, and Nestor behind to guard the ships.

When news was brought to King Laomedon that the Greek fleet had landed at Sigeum, he took command of the cavalry himself and went to the shore and opened hostilities.

But Hercules, having gone on to Troy, was beginning to besiege the unsuspecting inhabitants of the city. When Laomedon learned what was happening at home, he tried to return immediately. But the Greeks stood in his way, and Hercules slew him.

Telamon proved his prowess by being the first to enter Troy. Therefore, Hercules gave him the prize of King Laomedon's daughter Hesione.

Needless to say, all those who had gone with Laomedon were killed.

At this time Priam was in Phrygia, where Laomedon, his father, had put him in charge of the army.[3]

Hercules and those who had come with him plundered the country and carried much booty off to their ships. Then they decided to set out for home. Telamon took Hesione with him. |4| When news was brought to Priam that his father had been killed, his fellow-citizens decimated, his country plundered, and his sister Hesione carried off as a prize of war, he was deeply upset to think that the Greeks had treated Phrygia with such contempt. He returned to Troy, along with his wife, Hecuba, and his children, Hector, Alexander, Deiphobus, Helenus, Troilus, Andromache, Cassandra, and Polyxena. (He had other sons by concubines, but only those by lawfully wedded wives could claim a truly royal lineage.) Arriving in Troy, he saw to the maximum fortification of the city, built stronger walls, and stationed a greater number of soldiers nearby. Troy must not fall again, as it had under his father, Laomedon, through lack of preparedness.

He also constructed a palace, in which he consecrated an altar and statue to Jupiter; sent Hector into Paeonia; and built the gates of Troy—the Antenorean, the Dardanian, the Ilian, the Scaean, the Thymbraean, and the Trojan.

When he saw that Troy was secure, he waited until the time seemed right to avenge the wrongs his father had suffered. Then he summoned Antenor and told him he wished him to go as an envoy to Greece. The Greek army, he said, had done him grave wrongs by killing his father, Laomedon, and by carrying off Hesione. Nevertheless, if only Hesione were returned, he would cease to complain.

|5| In obedience to Priam's command, Antenor boarded a ship and sailed to Magnesia to visit Peleus. For three days Peleus entertained him hospitably, and on the fourth asked why he had come. Antenor, following Priam's instructions, said that he had come to demand that the Greeks return Hesione. On hearing this, Peleus was deeply upset, and since he saw that this was a matter which touched his interests[4] he ordered Antenor to depart from his boundaries.

Antenor, without any delay whatsoever, boarded his ship and, sailing along past Boeotia, came to the island of Salamis. There he tried to persuade Telamon to return to Priam his sister Hesione. It was not right, he said, to hold a girl of royal rank in servitude. Telamon answered that he had committed no wrong against Priam. He refused to return her whom he had received as a prize of war and ordered Antenor to depart from his island.

Antenor, having boarded his ship, went on to Achaea. There he was taken to Castor and Pollux and tried to persuade them to make reparation to Priam by returning his sister Hesione. Castor and Pollux denied that Priam had suffered any injury and ordered Antenor to depart.

Then he went to Pylos and told Nestor the purpose of his mission. When Nestor knew why he had come, he began to scold him. How, he asked, had he dared to undertake this mission? The Phrygians had been the first to offend.

When Antenor saw that he was accomplishing nothing, but

that he was being treated with scorn, he boarded his ship and returned to his homeland. Reporting to Priam, he told what each one had said and how each one had treated him; and he urged the king to make war.

|6| Immediately Priam summoned his sons and all of his friends —Antenor, Anchises, Aeneas, Ucalegon, Bucolion, Panthus, and Lampus—and all of the sons he had fathered by concubines. When they had come, he told them about Antenor's unsuccessful mission, how he had gone to Greece and demanded as satisfaction for Laomedon's death the return of Hesione; and how the Greeks had treated him scornfully and sent him home empty-handed. Now, Priam concluded, since the Greeks refused to do as he wished, he would send an army to make them pay for their crimes, lest they think barbarians worthy of scorn. And he urged his sons —especially Hector since he was the oldest—to take command of the forces.

Hector responded by saying that he would carry out his father's wishes and avenge the death of his grandfather, Laomedon, and the other injustices the Greeks had done to the Trojans. The Greeks, he said, must pay for their crimes. He feared, however, that the Trojan expedition would fail, for Europe had bred many warlike men who would come to Greece's aid, while they themselves, who lived in Asia, had spent their time in idleness and built no ships.

|7| Then Alexander began to exhort them. They must build a fleet and go against Greece. If his father wished, he would take charge of this venture; he would conquer the enemy and return from Greece with great renown. There was reason to believe that the gods would aid him, for, while hunting in the woods on Mount Ida, he had fallen asleep and dreamt as follows:

Mercury brought Juno, Venus, and Minerva to him to judge of their beauty. Then Venus promised, if he judged her most beautiful, to give him in marriage whoever was deemed the loveliest woman in Greece. Thus, finally, on hearing Venus' promise, he judged her most beautiful.

This dream inspired Priam with the hope that Venus would aid Alexander. And Deiphobus approved of what Alexander had said. He believed that the Greeks would return Hesione and make reparations if, as had been proposed, they would send a fleet against Greece.

Helenus, however, began to predict that if Alexander brought home a Greek wife, the Greeks would pursue, and overpower Troy and slay—oh cruel might—his parents and brothers.

But Troilus, who, though youngest of Priam's sons, equalled Hector in bravery, urged them to war and told them not to be frightened by Helenus' fearful words.

And so they unanimously decided to ready a fleet and set out for Greece.

|8| Priam sent Alexander and Deiphobus into Paeonia to raise an army.

Then he called the people to assembly. Having arranged a line of command beginning with his older and ending with his younger sons, he told how the Greeks had wronged the Trojans. He had sent Antenor as an envoy to Greece to regain his sister Hesione and obtain reparation for the Trojans, but the Greeks had treated Antenor scornfully and sent him home empty-handed. For this reason he had decided to send Alexander with a fleet against Greece. Thus Alexander would avenge the death of his grandfather and the other wrongs that the Trojans had suffered.

Then Priam ordered Antenor to tell how he had been treated in Greece. Antenor briefly described his mission and, urging the Trojans to have no fear, made them more eager for war against Greece.

Then Priam asked for other opinions: Would anyone like to speak against war?

Thereupon Panthus, addressing himself to the king and his

party, told what he had heard from his father, Euphorbus: If Alexander brought home a wife from Greece, Troy would utterly fall. It was much better, he said, to spend one's life in peace than to risk the loss of liberty in war.

Panthus' speech won the contempt of the people, and they asked the king what had to be done. When he told them that they must build ships to go against Greece and gather supplies for the army, they cried out that they were ready to obey any order he gave them. For this he thanked them profusely, and then dismissed the assembly.

Soon afterwards he ordered men to go to the forests of Ida and there cut wood for building the ships; and he sent Hector into Upper Phrygia to levy an army.

When Cassandra heard of her father's intentions, she told what the Trojans were going to suffer if Priam should send a fleet into Greece.

|9| Soon preparations were made. The ships were built, and the army which Alexander and Deiphobus had raised in Paeonia had come. When the time seemed right for sailing, Priam addressed the troops. He appointed Alexander as commander-in-chief, and made Deiphobus, Aeneas, and Polydamas officers. First, he said, Alexander must go to Sparta and ask Castor and Pollux to return his sister Hesione, and to make reparations to the Trojans. Then, if Castor and Pollux refused, Alexander must send home word immediately. Thus he, Priam, would feel able to order the army to go against Greece.

Accordingly, Alexander sailed for Greece, piloted by the same man who had gone with Antenor. Several days before they reached Greece—before they came to the island of Cythera—they passed Menelaus, who was on his way to visit Nestor at Pylos. Menelaus marveled at the royal fleet and wondered where it was heading. In fact, each party, surprised at seeing the other, wondered where the other was going.

Castor and Pollux had gone to visit Clytemnestra at Argos,

where the festival of Juno was being held; and they had taken along their niece Hermione, the daughter of Helen.

It was at this time that Alexander arrived on Cythera and sacrificed to Diana at a place where the temple of Venus was.[5] The inhabitants of the island marveled at the royal fleet and asked the sailors who they were and why they had come. They answered that King Priam was sending Alexander to confer with Castor and Pollux.

|10| While Alexander was on Cythera, Helen, the wife of Menelaus, decided to go there. Thus she went to the shore, to the seaport town of Helaea,[6] intending to worship in the temple of Diana and Apollo.[7] Alexander, on hearing that she had arrived, wanted to see her. Confident in his own good looks, he began to walk within sight of her. When Helen learned that the Alexander who was the son of King Priam had come to Helaea, she also wanted to see him. Thus they met and spent some time just staring, struck by each other's beauty.

Alexander ordered his men to be ready to sail that night. They would seize Helen in the temple and take her home with them.

Thus at a given signal they invaded the temple and carried her off—she was not unwilling—along with some other women they captured. The inhabitants of the town, having learned about the abduction of Helen, tried to prevent Alexander from carrying her off. They fought long and hard, but Alexander's superior forces defeated them. After despoiling the temple and taking as many captives as his ships would hold, he set sail for home.

On the island of Tenedos, where they landed, he tried to comfort Helen, who was having regrets; and he sent news to his father of his success.

Menelaus, having learned what had happened, left Pylos accompanied by Nestor, and returned to Sparta whither he summoned his brother Agamemnon from Argos.[8]

|11| Meanwhile Alexander arrived home with his booty and gave

his father an exact description of everything he had done. Priam was delighted. He hoped that the Greeks would seek to recover Helen, and thus would return his sister Hesione,[9] and the things they had taken from Troy. He consoled Helen, who was having regrets, and gave her to Alexander to marry. When Cassandra saw Helen, she began to prophesy, repeating what she had already said; until Priam ordered her carried away and locked up.

Agamemnon, upon his arrival in Sparta, consoled his brother. They decided to send men throughout Greece to gather an army for war against Troy. Among those who assembled at Sparta were Achilles, who came with Patroclus; and Euryalus, Tlepolemus, and Diomedes. They swore to avenge the wrongs the Trojans had done and to ready an army and fleet for this purpose. Agamemnon was chosen commander-in-chief, and messengers were sent to summon all the Greeks to the Athenian port with their ships and armies. From there they would set out for Troy together to avenge the wrongs they had suffered.

Castor and Pollux, immediately upon learning of their sister Helen's abduction, had set sail in pursuit.[10] When, however, they landed on the island of Lesbos, a great storm arose and, lo and behold, they were nowhere in sight. That was the story. Later, people thought that they had been made immortal. The Lesbians, taking to the sea and searching even to Troy, had returned to report that they had found no trace of Castor or Pollux.

|12| Dares the Phrygian, who wrote this history, says that he did military service until the capture of Troy and saw the people listed below either during times of truce or while he was fighting.[11] As for Castor and Pollux, he learned from the Trojans what they were like and how they looked: they were twins, blond haired, large eyed, fair complexioned, and wellbuilt with trim bodies.[12]

Helen resembled Castor and Pollux.[13] She was beautiful, ingenuous, and charming. Her legs were the best; her mouth the cutest. There was a beauty-mark between her eyebrows.

Priam, the king of the Trojans, had a handsome face and a pleasant voice. He was large and swarthy.

Hector spoke with a slight lisp. His complexion was fair, his hair curly. His eyes would blink attractively. His movements were swift. His face, with its beard, was noble. He was handsome, fierce, and high-spirited, merciful to the citizens, and deserving of love.

Deiphobus and Helenus both looked like their father, but their characters were not alike. Deiphobus was the man of forceful action; Helenus was the gentle, learned prophet.

Troilus, a large and handsome boy, was strong for his age, brave, and eager for glory.

Alexander was fair, tall, and brave. His eyes were very beautiful, his hair soft and blond, his mouth charming, and his voice pleasant. He was swift, and eager to take command.

Aeneas was auburn-haired, stocky, eloquent, courteous, prudent, pious, and charming. His eyes were black and twinkling.

Antenor was tall, graceful, swift, crafty, and cautious.

Hecuba was beautiful, her figure large, her complexion dark. She thought like a man and was pious and just.

Andromache was bright-eyed and fair, with a tall and beautiful body. She was modest, wise, chaste, and charming.

Cassandra was of moderate stature, round-mouthed, and auburn-haired. Her eyes flashed. She knew the future.

Polyxena was fair, tall, and beautiful. Her neck was slender, her eyes lovely, her hair blond and long, her body well-proportioned, her fingers tapering, her legs straight, and her feet the best. Surpassing all the others in beauty, she remained a completely ingenuous and kind-hearted woman.

|13| Agamemnon was blond, large, and powerful. He was eloquent, wise, and noble, a man richly endowed.

Menelaus was of moderate stature, auburn-haired, and handsome. He had a pleasing personality.

Achilles had a large chest, a fine mouth, and powerfully formed arms and legs. His head was covered with long wavy chestnut-colored hair. Though mild in manner, he was very fierce in battle. His face showed the joy of a man richly endowed.

Patroclus was handsome and powerfully built. His eyes were gray. He was modest, dependable, wise, a man richly endowed.

Ajax, the son of Oileus, was stocky, powerfully built, swarthy a pleasant person, and brave.

Ajax, the son of Telamon, was powerful. His voice was clear, his hair black and curly. He was perfectly single-minded and unrelenting in the onslaught of battle.

Ulysses was tough, crafty, cheerful, of medium height, elrquent, and wise.

Diomedes was stocky, brave, dignified, and austere. No one was fiercer in battle. He was loud at the war cry, hot-tempered, impatient, and daring.

Nestor was large, broad, and fair. His nose was long and hooked. He was the wise adviser.

Protesilaus was fair-skinned, and dignified. He was swift, self-confident, even rash.

Neoptolemus was large, robust, and easily irritated. He lisped slightly, and was good-looking, with hooked nose, round eyes, and shaggy eyebrows.

Palamedes was tall and slender, wise, magnanimous, and charming.

Podalirius was sturdy, strong, haughty, and moody.

Machaon was large and brave, dependable, prudent, patient, and merciful.

Meriones was auburn-haired, of moderate height, with a well-proportioned body. He was robust, swift, unmerciful, and easily angered.

Briseis was beautiful. She was small and blond, with soft yellow hair. Her eyebrows were joined above her lovely eyes.

Her body was well-proportioned. She was charming, friendly, modest, ingenuous, and pious.

|14| The following is a list of Greek leaders and the ships they brought to Athens.[14] Agamemnon came from Mycenae with 100 ships; Menelaus from Sparta with 60; Arcesilaus and Prothoenor from Boeotia with 50; Ascalaphus and Ialmenus from Orchomenus with 30; Epistrophus and Schedius from Phocis with 40; Ajax the son of Telamon brought along Teucer, his brother, from Salamis, and also Amphimachus, Diores, Thalpius, and Polyxenus from Buprasion, with 40 ships; Nestor came from Pylos with 80; Thoas from Aetolia with 40; Nireus from Syme with 53; Ajax the son of Oileus from Locris with 37; Antiphus and Phidippus from Calydna with 30; Idomeneus and Meriones from Crete with 80; Ulysses from Ithaca with 12; Eumelus from Pherae with 10; Protesilaus and Podarces from Phylaca with 40; Podalirius and Machaon, the sons of Aesculapius, from Tricca with 32; Achilles, accompanied by Patroclus and the Myrmidons, from Phthia with 50; Tlepolemus from Rhodes with 9; Eurypylus from Ormenion with 40; Antiphus and Amphimachus from Elis with 11; Polypoetes and Leonteus from Argisa with 40; Diomedes, Euryalus, and Sthenelus from Argos with 80; Philoctetes from Meliboea with 7; Guneus from Cyphos with 21; Prothous from Magnesia with 40; Agapenor from Arcadia with 40; and Menestheus from Athens with 50. There were 49 Greek leaders, and they brought a total of 1,130 ships.

|15| When they had arrived at Athens, Agamemnon called the leaders to council. He praised them and urged them to avenge the wrongs they had suffered as quickly as possible. Let each one, he said, tell how he felt. Then he advised that, before setting sail, they should consult the oracle of Apollo at Delphi. The council agreed unanimously and appointed Achilles to be in charge of this mission; and thus he, along with Patroclus, set out to Delphi.

Meanwhile Priam, having learned that the Greeks were preparing for war, sent men throughout Phrygia to enlist the support of the neighboring armies. He himself zealously readied his forces at home.

When Achilles had come to Delphi, he went to the oracle. The response, which issued from the holiest of holies, said that the Greeks would conquer and capture Troy in the tenth year. Then Achilles performed his religious duties as ordered.

At the same time the seer Calchas, the son of Thestor, had arrived, sent by his people, the Phrygians, to bring gifts to Apollo. When he inquiring in behalf of his kingdom and of himself consulted the oracle, the response which issued from the holiest of holies said that the Greeks would sail against Troy and would continue their siege until they had captured it, and that he would go with them and give them advice.

Thus Achilles and Calchas met in the temple and, after comparing responses, rejoiced in each other's friendship and set out for Athens together.

At Athens Achilles made his report to the council. The Greeks were delighted. And they accepted Calchas as one of their own.

Then they set sail. But a storm arose and prevented their progress. Thereupon Calchas, interpreting the omens, said that they must return and go up to Aulis.

On arriving at Aulis, Agamemnon appeased the goddess Diana. Then he commanded his followers to sail onwards to Troy. Philoctetes, who had gone with the Argonauts to Troy, acted as pilot.[15]

Then they landed at a city which was ruled by King Priam. They took it by storm and carried off much booty.

On coming to the island of Tenedos, they killed all the people, and Agamemnon divided the booty.

|16| Then, having called a meeting of the council, he sent envoys to Priam to ask for the return of Helen and the booty Alexander

had taken; Diomedes and Ulysses were chosen to go on this mission. At the same time Achilles and Telephus were sent to plunder Mysia, the region ruled by King Teuthras.[16]

They had come to this region and had begun to despoil the country when Teuthras arrived with his army. Thereupon Achilles put the enemy to flight, and also wounded the king. He would have finished him off if Telephus had not stood in his way. Telephus came to Teuthras' aid and protected him under his shield, for he remembered their friendship, the time in his boyhood when Teuthras had been his generous host: Teuthras had felt indebted to Telephus' father, Hercules, for Hercules, so they said, had slain Diomedes, the previous king of Mysia, from whom Teuthras had inherited the kingdom. (Diomedes had met his death while hunting with his wild and powerful horses.) Nevertheless, now Teuthras realized that he was unable to live much longer, and so he appointed Telephus heir to the throne and king of Mysia.

Telephus held a magnificent funeral for Teuthras. Then Achilles urged him to stay behind and take care of his newly gained kingdom. Telephus, he said, would aid the Greeks much more by sending supplies than by going to Troy. Thus Telephus stayed behind in his kingdom, and Achilles, carrying much booty, returned to the army on Tenedos. His report of what had been done won Agamemnon's approval and praise.

|17| Meanwhile the envoys had come to Priam, and Ulysses stated Agamemnon's demands. If Helen and the booty, he said, were returned and proper reparations were made, the Greeks would depart in peace.

Priam answered by reviewing the wrongs the Argonauts had done:[17] the death of his father, the sack of Troy, and the capture of his sister Hesione. He ended by describing how contemptuously the Greeks had treated Antenor when sent as his envoy. He, therefore, repudiated peace. He declared war and commanded that the envoys of the Greeks be expelled from his boundaries.

Thus the envoys returned to their camp on Tenedos and reported what Priam had answered. And the council discussed what to do.

|18| This seems to be a good place to list the leaders who brought armies to aid King Priam against the Greeks and to tell the countries from which they came.[18] Pandarus, Amphius, and Adrastus came from Zelia; Mopsus from Colophon; Asius from Phrygia; Amphimachus and Nastes from Caria; Sarpedon and Glaucus from Lycia; Hippothous and Cupesus from Larissa; Euphemus from Ciconia; Pirus and Acamas from Thrace; Pyraechmes and Asteropaeus from Paeonia; Ascanius and Phorcys from Phrygia; Antiphus and Mesthles from Maeonia; Pylaemenes from Paphlagonia; Perses and Memnon from Ethiopia; Rhesus and Archilochus from Thrace; Adrastus and Amphius from Adrestia; and Epistrophus and Odius from Alizonia. Priam made Hector commander-in-chief of these leaders and their armies. Second-in-command were Deiphobus, Alexander, Troilus, Aeneas, and Memnon.

While Agamemnon was making his plans complete, Palamedes, the son of Nauplius, arrived with thirty ships from Cormos.[19] He had been incapacitated by sickness from coming to Athens and begged their pardon. They thanked him for coming when he was able and asked him to share in their counsels.

|19| The Greeks debated whether they should make their attack against Troy secretly at night or during the day. Palamedes urged them to land by day, for thus they would draw the enemy forces out of the city. His advice was accepted unanimously. Then they decided to give Agamemnon command; and three envoys were appointed to gather supplies in Mysia and other places: Anius[20] and the two sons of Theseus, Demophoon and Acamas.

Then Agamemnon, having called the soldiers to assembly, praised them and demanded their immediate and total allegiance.

When the signal was given, the ships set sail and landed at

Troy, with the whole fleet widely deployed. The Trojans bravely defended their country. Hector met and slew Protesilaus and caused great confusion among the rest of the Greeks.[21] (Protesilaus had gone inland, wreaking slaughter and putting the Trojans to flight.) But wherever Hector withdrew, the Trojans fled. The losses on both sides were heavy until the arrival of Achilles caused all the Trojans to flee back to Troy. When night brought an end to the battle, Agamemnon led forth all of his army onto the land and set up camp.

On the next day Hector led forth his army out of the city ready for battle. Agamemnon's forces moved opposite, shouting their war cry. The battle that arose was fierce and raging; the bravest of those who fought in the vanguard fell. Hector slew Patroclus; he was trying to strip off his armor when Meriones snatched the body out of the action. Then Hector pursued and cut down Meriones. This time, however, while trying to despoil the body, he was wounded in the leg by Menestheus, who had come to the aid of his comrade. Hector, though wounded, slew a great number of the enemy and would have successfully turned the Greek forces to flight had Ajax the son of Telamon not stood in his way. Immediately upon meeting Ajax, Hector remembered that they were related: Ajax' mother was Priam's sister Hesione. Therefore, he commanded the Trojans to stop setting fire to the ships. And then the two men gave gifts to each other and departed in friendship.[22]

|20| On the next day the Greeks obtained a truce.[23] Achilles mourned for Patroclus, and the Greeks for their dead. Agamemnon held a magnificent funeral for Protesilaus and saw to the proper burial of the others. And Achilles celebrated funeral games in honor of Patroclus.

During this truce Palamedes continuously pressed for sedition. King Agamemnon, he said, ill deserved the command of the army. Palamedes openly boasted of his own numerous accomplishments, particularly his tactics on offense, his fortifications of the camp, his regulation of guard duty, his invention of signals and scales, and his training of the army for battle. These things were due to him, and it was therefore not right, he said, for Agamemnon, whom only a few had chosen as leader, to command all those who had joined the campaign later. All of them had a right to expect a man who was brilliant and brave in this position.

After two years, during which time the Greeks debated who should command them, the war was resumed. Agamemnon, Achilles, Diomedes, and Menelaus led forth their army. The forces of Hector, Troilus, and Aeneas moved opposite. A great slaughter arose, and many very brave men fell on both sides. Hector slew Boetes, Arcesilaus, and Prothoenor. When night brought an end to the battle, Agamemnon called all the leaders to council and urged them to enter the fray and try to kill Hector especially, for Hector had slain some of their bravest commanders. |21| With the coming of morning, Hector, Aeneas, and Alexander led forth their army. And all the Greek leaders advanced with their forces. A great slaughter arose, and on both sides countless numbers were sent down to Orcus.[24] Menelaus began to pursue Alexander who, turning around, pierced him in the leg with an arrow. Nevertheless, though pained by his wound, Menelaus continued to pursue, and Locrian Ajax accompanied him. Hector saw what was happening, and immediately he and Aeneas came to the aid of their brother. While Aeneas, using his shield, provided protection, Hector led Alexander out of the fighting and into the city.[25] Night brought an end to the battle.

On the next day Achilles and Diomedes led forth their army. The forces of Hector and Aeneas came opposite. A great slaughter arose. Hector slew the leaders Orcomeneus, Ialmenus, Epistrophus, Schedius, Elephenor, Diores, and Polyxenus. Aeneas slew Amphimachus and Nireus. Achilles slew Euphemus, Hippothous, Pylaeus, and Asteropaeus. And Diomedes slew Antiphus and

Mesthles. When Agamemnon saw that his bravest leaders had fallen, he called back his forces; and the Trojans returned to their city, rejoicing. Agamemnon was worried. Calling the leaders to council, he urged them to fight on bravely and not to give way. More than half of their forces had fallen, but any day now an army was coming from Mysia.

|22| On the next day Agamemnon ordered the whole army, with all of the leaders, to go forth to battle. The Trojans came opposite. A great slaughter arose, with both sides battling fiercely and losing countless numbers of men, there being no break in the fighting, which raged for eighty consecutive days. Agamemnon, seeing the steadily mounting casualties, felt that time was needed for burying the dead. Therefore, he sent Ulysses and Diomedes as envoys to Priam to seek a truce of three years. During this time the Greeks would also be able to heal their wounded, repair the ships, reinforce the army, and gather supplies.

Ulysses and Diomedes, while on their way to Priam by dark, met a Trojan named Dolon. When he asked why they were coming to the city, in arms and at night, they told him that they were envoys from Agamemnon to Priam.[26]

When Priam heard of their coming and knew what they wanted, he called all of his leaders to council. Then he announced that these were envoys Agamemnon had sent to seek a truce of three years. Hector suspected something was wrong. They wanted, he said, a truce for too long a time. Nevertheless, when Priam ordered the members of the council to give their opinions, they voted to grant a truce of three years.

During the truce the Trojans repaired their walls, healed their wounded, and buried their dead with great honor.

|23| After three years, the war was resumed. Hector and Troilus led forth their army. Agamemnon, Menelaus, Achilles, and Diomedes commanded the Greeks. A great slaughter arose, with Hector killing the leaders of the first rank, Phidippus and Anti-

phus, and Achilles slaying Lycaon and Phorcys. Countless numbers of others fell on both sides, as the battle raged for thirty con-
secutive days. Priam, seeing that many of his men were falling,
sent envoys to seek a truce of six months. This Agamemnon, following the will of his council, conceded.

With the resumption of hostilities, the battle raged for twelve
days. On both sides many of the bravest leaders fell; and even
more were wounded, a majority of whom died during treatment.
Therefore, Agamemnon sent envoys to Priam to seek a thirty-day
truce for burying the dead. Priam, after consulting his council,
agreed.

|24| When time for fighting returned, Andromache, Hector's
wife, had a dream which forbade Hector to enter the fray. He,
however, dismissed this vision as due to her wifely concern. She,
being deeply upset, sent word to Priam to keep her husband out
of the battle that day. Priam, therefore, divided the command of
his forces between Alexander, Helenus, Troilus, and Aeneas. Hector, on learning of this, bitterly blamed Andromache and told her
to bring forth his armor; nothing, he said, could keep him from
battle. She tried in vain to make him relent, falling at his feet, like
a woman in mourning, her hair let down, holding the baby, their
son Astyanax, out in her hands. Then, rushing to the palace, her
wailing rousing the city as she went, she told King Priam how she
had dreamt that Hector would eagerly leap into battle; and, holding Astyanax, she knelt before him and begged him not to allow
this. Accordingly, Priam sent all the others to battle, but kept
Hector back.

When Agamemnon, Achilles, Diomedes, and the Locrian
Ajax saw that Hector was not on the field, they fought the more
fiercely, slaying many leaders of the Trojans. But Hector, hearing the tumult and knowing that the Trojans were being hard
pressed, leaped into battle. Immediately he slew Idomeneus,
wounded Iphinous, cut down Leonteus, and thrust a spear into

Sthenelus' leg. Achilles, seeing these leaders fall and wanting to prevent other Greeks from meeting a similar fate, determined to go against Hector and slay him. But by the time he caught up with Hector, the battle continuing to rage, the latter had already killed Polypoetes, the bravest of leaders, and was trying to strip off the armor. The fight that arose was terrific, as was the clamor from city and armies. Hector wounded Achilles' leg. But Achilles, though pained, pressed on all the harder and kept pressing on until he had won. Hector's death caused the Trojans to turn and flee for their gates, their numbers greatly depleted. Only Memnon resisted. He and Achilles fought fiercely, and neither got off without injuries. When night brought an end to the battle, the wounded Achilles returned to camp. The Trojans lamented for Hector, and the Greeks for their dead.

|25| On the next day Memnon led forth the Trojans against the Greeks. Agamemnon, having called the army to assembly, urged a truce of two months for burying the dead. Thus envoys set out for Troy, and there, having told what they wanted to Priam, received a truce of two months.

Then Priam, following the custom of his people, buried Hector in front of the gates and held funeral games in his honor.

During the truce, Palamedes continued to complain about the Greek leadership, and so Agamemnon yielded to sedition. He said that the Greeks might choose as their general whomever they wished, so far as he cared.

On the next day he called the people to assembly and denied he had ever wanted to command them. He was ready to accept whomever they chose. He willingly yielded. All he desired was to punish the enemy, and it mattered little how this was done. Nevertheless, as he was still king of Mycenae, he commanded them to speak as they wished.

Then Palamedes came forward and, showing his qualifications, won the acclaim of the Greeks. They made him commander-in-chief, a position he gratefully accepted and began to administer. Achilles, however, disparaged the change.

|26| When the truce was over, Palamedes, arranging his forces and urging them on, led forth the army ready for battle. Deiphobus commanded the Trojans, who offered fierce opposition. The Lycian Sarpedon, leading his men, attacked and caused great slaughter and havoc. The Rhodian Tlepolemus met and resisted Sarpedon, but finally fell badly wounded. Then Pheres, the son of Admetus, came up and, after a long hand-to-hand fight with Sarpedon, was killed. But Sarpedon also was wounded and forced from the battle. Thus for several days there was fighting, and many leaders died on both sides. The Trojan casualties, however, were greater. When they sent envoys to seek a respite for burying their dead and healing their wounded, Palamedes granted a truce of one year.

Both sides buried their dead and cared for their wounded. Their agreement allowed them to go to each other's areas; the Trojans went to the camp, the Greeks to the city.

Palamedes sent Agamemnon to Mysia to Acamas and Demophoon, Theseus' sons, whom Agamemnon had put in charge of bringing supplies and grain from Telephus. Upon his arrival in Mysia, Agamemnon told them about Palamedes' sedition. When, however, he saw that they were displeased, he admitted that he had agreed to the change.

Meanwhile Palamedes was readying the ships and fortifying the camp with walls and towers. The Trojans were training their army, repairing their walls, adding a rampart and ditch, and diligently getting everything ready.

|27| On the first anniversary of Hector's funeral, Priam, Hecuba, Polyxena, and other Trojans went to the tomb. There they happened to meet Achilles, who, being struck by Polyxena's beauty, fell madly in love. The burning power of his love took all the joy out of life. (His soul was also rankled by the fact that the

Greeks had deposed Agamemnon and made Palamedes commander-in-chief instead of himself.) Accordingly, urged by his love, he sent a trusted Phrygian slave to make this proposal to Hecuba: if she would give him Polyxena to marry, he would go home with his Myrmidons, and thus would set an example which the other leaders would follow. When the slave went to Hecuba and made this proposal, she answered that she would be willing, if Priam agreed, but that she must talk with him first. Then the slave, as Hecuba ordered, returned to Achilles and told him her answer.

Agamemnon, coming from Mysia with a large group of followers, arrived in camp at this time.

When Hecuba talked to Priam about Achilles' proposal, Priam refused to agree. Granted that Achilles would make a good relative, it was not right to marry one's daughter to an enemy; and even if Achilles himself went home, the other Greeks would not follow. Therefore, if Achilles wanted this marriage, he must promise a lasting peace, a treaty with sacred oaths; and the Greeks must depart. On these conditions, Priam would willingly give him his daughter in marriage.

The slave of Achilles, according to his understanding with Hecuba, returned to her and learned what Priam had said. Then he reported all he had heard back to his master. Thereupon Achilles complained, to any and everyone, that for the sake of one woman, that is, Helen, all Europe and Greece were in arms, and now, for a very long time, thousands of men had been dying. Their very liberty, he said, was at stake, and this was the reason they ought to make peace and take their army back home.

|28| When the year was over, Palamedes led forth the army and drew it up. And the Trojans came opposite commanded by Deiphobus. (Achilles, however, refused to take part because of his anger.) Palamedes seized an opportunity to attack Deiphobus and slaughtered him.

A fierce battle arose, fiercely fought on both sides; there were countless numbers of casualties. Palamedes, active in the first ranks, urging his men to fight bravely, encountered and slew the Lycian Sarpedon. But as he continued to prowl in the vanguard, spurred on by success, exulting, and vaunting his prowess, Alexander (Paris) pierced his neck with an arrow; and then the Phrygians, seeing their chance, hurled their spears and finished him off. King Palamedes was dead. Accordingly, all the Trojans attacked. They pursued the Greeks, and the Greeks retreated and fled to the camp. The camp was besieged, the ships set on fire.

Achilles, though told what was happening, chose to pretend that things were all right.

Ajax the son of Telamon bravely led the defense until night brought an end to the battle. Then the Greeks lamented the loss of Palamedes' wisdom, justice, mercy, and goodness; and the Trojans bewailed the deaths of Sarpedon and Deiphobus.

|29| Also during this night Nestor, since he was the eldest, called the Greek leaders to council and, speaking with tact, urged them to choose a new general. He felt that, if they thought best, Agamemnon's reappointment would cause the least discord. He reminded them that while Agamemnon was general things had gone well and the army had prospered. If, however, anyone had a better idea, he urged him to speak. But all, agreeing with him, made Agamemnon commander-in-chief.

On the next day the Trojans quickly came forth. And Agamemnon led the Greeks opposite. The battle was joined, and the two forces clashed. Towards evening Troilus advanced to the front and, wreaking slaughter and havoc, sent the Greeks flying back to their camp.

On the next day the Trojans led forth their army. And the forces of Agamemnon came opposite. A horrible slaughter arose. Both armies fought fiercely; Troilus slaughtered many Greek leaders, as the battle lasted seven days.

Then Agamemnon, having obtained a truce of two months,

held a magnificent funeral in Palamedes' honor. Both sides saw to the burial of all the leaders and soldiers who had died.

|30| During the truce, Agamemnon sent Ulysses, Nestor, and Diomedes to Achilles to ask him to reenter the fighting. But Achilles, still moody, refused to budge from his decision to stay out of battle. He told about his promise to Hecuba and said that he would certainly fight rather poorly because of his passionate love for Polyxena. They whom Agamemnon had sent were not welcome. A lasting peace—that was the need. For the sake of one woman, he said, the Greeks were risking their lives, endangering their freedom, and wasting a great deal of time. Thus Achilles demanded peace, and refused to reenter the fighting.

When Agamemnon learned of Achilles' stubborn refusal, he summoned all the leaders to council and asked them to tell what they thought should be done.

Menelaus urged Agamemnon to lead the army to battle and not to worry about the withdrawal of Achilles. He himself would try to win over Achilles, but if he should fail, he would not be dejected. Furthermore, he said, the Trojans now had no one to take Hector's place, no one so brave.

Diomedes and Ulysses answered that Troilus was the bravest of men and the equal of Hector.

But Menelaus denied this and urged the council to continue the war.

Calchas, taking the omens, informed them that they ought to do battle and not be frightened by the Trojans' recent successes.

|31| When the time for fighting returned, Agamemnon, Menelaus, and Ajax led forth the army. The Trojans came opposite. A great slaughter arose, a fierce and raging battle on both sides. Troilus, having wounded Menelaus, pressed on, killing many of the enemy and harrying the others. Night brought an end to the battle.

On the next day Troilus and Alexander led forth the Trojans. And all the Greeks came opposite. The battle was fierce. Troilus wounded Diomedes and, in the course of his slaughter, attacked and wounded Agamemnon himself.

For several days the battle raged on. Countless numbers fell on both sides. Then Agamemnon, seeing that he was losing more of his forces each day, and knowing that they were unable to last, sought a truce of six months.

Priam, having called a meeting of his council, reported the desires of the Greeks. Troilus felt that they were asking for too long a time; he urged the Trojans to continue fighting, and fire the ships. When, however, Priam ordered the members of the council to give their opinions, the vote was unanimous in favor of the Greek petition, and thus they granted a truce of six months.

Agamemnon buried his dead with honors and saw to the care of the wounded, such as Diomedes and Menelaus. The Trojans also buried their dead.

During the truce Agamemnon, following the advice of his council, went to rouse Achilles to battle. But Achilles, still gloomy, refused to go forth; he felt that the king should be suing for peace. Nevertheless, after complaining that it was impossible to refuse Agamemnon, he said that he would send forth his forces when war was resumed, though he himself would stay back. For this Agamemnon gave him his thanks.

|32| When the time for war returned, the Trojans led forth their army. And the forces of the Greeks came opposite. Achilles, having drawn up his Myrmidons, sent them to Agamemnon ready for combat. A great battle arose, fierce and raging. Troilus, fighting in the first ranks, slaughtered the Greeks and put the Myrmidons to flight. He pressed his attack even into the camp, killing many and wounding most who stood in his way until Ajax the son of Telamon stopped him. The Trojans returned to the city victorious.

On the next day Agamemnon led forth his army along with

the Myrmidons and all of his leaders. And the Trojans came opposite, eager to fight. The battle was joined. For several days both sides fought fiercely, and countless numbers were lost. Troilus, attacking the Myrmidons and breaking their order, put them to flight.

When Agamemnon saw that many of his men had been killed, he sought a thirty-day truce for holding their funerals. This was granted by Priam, and thus the Greeks and Trojans buried their dead.

|33| When the time for war returned, the Trojans led forth their army. And Agamemnon came opposite with all of his leaders. The battle was joined. A great slaughter, fierce and raging, arose. When the morning had passed, Troilus advanced to the front, slaying the Greeks and making them flee with loud cries in general confusion. It was then that Achilles, seeing this mad and savage advance—the Greeks being crushed and the Myrmidons being relentlessly slaughtered—reentered the battle; but almost immediately he had to withdraw, wounded by Troilus. The others continued to fight for six days.

On the seventh, the battle still raging, Achilles (who until then had stayed out of action because of his wound) drew up his Myrmidons and urged them bravely to make an attack against Troilus. Toward the end of the day Troilus advanced on horseback, exulting, and caused the Greeks to flee with loud cries. The Myrmidons, however, came to their rescue and made an attack against Troilus. Troilus slew many men, but, in the midst of the terrible fighting, his horse was wounded and fell, entangling and throwing him off; and swiftly Achilles was there to dispatch him.

Then Achilles tried to drag off the body. But Memnon maintained a successful defense, wounding Achilles and making him yield. When, however, Memnon and his followers began to pursue Achilles, the latter, merely by turning around, brought them to halt.

After Achilles' wound had been dressed and he had fought

for some time, he slew Memnon, dealing him many a blow; and then, having been wounded himself, yielded from combat again. The rest of the Trojan forces, knowing that the king of the Persians was dead, fled to the city and bolted the gates. Night brought an end to the battle.

On the next day Priam sent envoys to Agamemnon to seek a twenty-day truce. This Agamemnon immediately granted. Accordingly, Priam held a magnificent funeral in honor of Troilus and Memnon. And both sides buried their dead.

|34| Hecuba, bewailing the loss of Hector and Troilus, her two bravest sons, both slain by Achilles, devised, like the woman she was, a treacherous vengeance. Summoning her son Alexander, she urgently begged him to kill Achilles, and thus to uphold the honor of himself and his brothers. This he could do in an ambush, catching his victim off guard. She would summon Achilles, in Priam's name, to come to the temple of the Thymbraean Apollo in front of the gate, to settle an agreement according to which she would give him Polyxena to marry. When Achilles came to this meeting, Alexander could treacherously kill him. Achilles' death would be victory sufficient for her.

Alexander promised to do as she asked. During that night he chose the bravest of the Trojans and stationed them in the temple with instructions to wait for his signal. Hecuba, as she had promised, sent word to Achilles. And Achilles, because of his love for Polyxena, gladly agreed to come to the temple that morning.

Accordingly, on the next day Achilles, along with Antilochus, Nestor's son, came for the meeting. Upon entering the temple, he was treacherously attacked. Spears were hurled from all sides, as Alexander exhorted his men. Achilles and Antilochus counterattacked, with their left arms wrapped in their cloaks for protection, their right hands wielding their swords; and Achilles slew many. But finally Alexander cut down Antilochus and then slaughtered Achilles, dealing him many a blow. Such was the death of this hero, a treacherous death and one ill-suiting his prowess.

Alexander's order to throw the bodies to the dogs and birds was countermanded by that of Helenus to take them out of the temple and hand them over to the Greeks. Thus the Greeks received their dead and carried them back to the camp. Agamemnon gave them magnificent funerals. He obtained a truce from Priam for the purpose of burying Achilles,[27] and then held funeral games in his honor.

|35| Then he called a meeting of the Greek council, at which he gave an address. It was unanimously decided that Achilles' command should be given to Ajax, who was Achilles' cousin. But Ajax objected that Neoptolemus, Achilles' son, was still living, and thus had first claim; therefore, they should bring Neoptolemus to Troy and give him command of the Myrmidons and all of his father's prerogatives.

Agamemnon and the rest of the council agreed and chose Menelaus to go on this mission.

When Menelaus had come to the island of Scyros, he urged King Lycomedes (Neoptolemus' grandfather) to send Neoptolemus to battle. The king gladly granted the Greeks this request.

The truce having come to an end, Agamemnon drew up his forces and, urging them on, led them to war. The Trojans came opposite out of the city. The battle was joined, with Ajax fighting up front, but wearing no armor. Great was the clamor that arose, and many died on both sides. Alexander, using his bow with frequent success, pierced the unarmed Ajax' body; Ajax, however, though wounded, pursued and finally killed his assailant. Then, as the wound had exhausted his strength, he was carried back to the camp; and there, though they drew out the arrow, he died.[28]

The Trojans, having rescued Alexander's body, fled back to the city, exhausted, before Diomedes' fierce onslaught. Diomedes pursued right up to the walls. Then Agamemnon, having ordered his forces to encircle the city, spent the whole night ready for battle, his guards always alerted.

On the next day, in the city, Priam buried Alexander. Helen took part in the funeral with loud lamentations. Alexander, she said, had treated her kindly; and thus she had become like a daughter to Priam and Hecuba, who always made her welcome at Troy and never let her remember her homeland.

|36| On the next day Agamemnon drew up his army in front of the gates and challenged the Trojans to come out and fight. But Priam stayed in the city, increasing his fortifications and waiting for Penthesilea to come with her Amazons.

When Penthesilea arrived, she led forth her army against Agamemnon. A huge battle arose. It raged several days, and then the Greeks, being overwhelmed, fled for their camp. Diomedes could hardly prevent Penthesilea from firing the ships and destroying all the Greek forces.

After this battle, Agamemnon kept his forces in camp. Penthesilea, to be sure, came forth each day and, slaughtering the Greeks, tried to provoke him to fight. But he, following the advice of his council, fortified the camp, strengthened the guard, and refused to go out to battle—until Menelaus arrived.

When, on Scyros, Menelaus had given Neoptolemus the arms of his father, Achilles, he brought him to join the Greeks at Troy. And here Neoptolemus wept and lamented above the tomb of his father.

Penthesilea, according to her custom, drew up her army and advanced as far as the camp of the Greeks. Neoptolemus, in command of the Myrmidons, led forth his forces. And Agamemnon drew up his army. Greeks and Trojans clashed head-on. Neoptolemus wreaked great slaughter. Penthesilea, having entered the fray, proved her prowess again and again.

For several days they fought fiercely, and many were killed.

Finally Penthesilea wounded Neoptolemus, and then fell at his hands; in spite of his wound, he cut her down.[29] The death of Penthesilea, the queen of the Amazons, caused all the Trojans to turn and flee in defeat for their city. And then the Greeks surrounded the walls with their forces and prevented anyone's leaving.

|37| When the Trojans saw their predicament, Antenor, Polydamas, and Aeneas went to Priam and asked him to call a meeting of the council to discuss the future of Troy and the Trojans.

Priam agreed, and so the meeting was called. Antenor spoke first, he and the other two having obtained permission to give their advice. The Trojans, he said, had lost their foremost defenders, Hector and the other sons of the king, along with the leaders from other places; but the Greeks still had their bravest commanders, Agamemnon, Menelaus, Neoptolemus, who was no less brave than his father, Diomedes, the Locrian Ajax, and many others besides, like Nestor and Ulysses, who were very shrewd men. Furthermore, the Trojans were surrounded and worn out with fear. Therefore, he urged the return of Helen and the things Alexander and his men had carried off with her. They must make peace.

After they had discussed making peace at some length, Amphimachus, Priam's son, a very brave youth, arose and, calling down curses upon Antenor and his associates, blamed them for the way they were acting.[30] He felt that the Trojans should lead forth their army and make an attack on the camp and never give up until they had either conquered or died fighting in behalf of their country.

After Amphimachus had spoken, Aeneas arose and tried to refute him. Speaking calmly and gently but with persistence, he urged the Trojans to sue for peace with the Greeks.

Then Polydamas urged the same course as Aeneas.

|38| After this speech Priam arose with great eagerness and

hurled many curses at Antenor and Aeneas. They had been the means, he said, by which war had arisen, for they were the envoys who had been sent to Greece; Antenor, who now urged peace, had then urged war when, on returning from Greece, he had told how scornfully he had been treated; and Aeneas had helped Alexander carry off Helen and the booty. In view of these facts, he, Priam, had made up his mind. There would be no peace.[31]

He commanded everyone to be prepared. When the signal was given, they must rush from the gates and either conquer or die. He had made up his mind.

After exhorting them thus at some length, Priam dismissed them. Then, taking Amphimachus along to the palace, he told him that those who urged peace must be killed. He feared that they would betray the city. Also, they had won much support for their views among the people. Once they were killed, he, Priam, would see to his country's defense and the Greeks' defeat.

Begging Amphimachus to be faithful and true, he told him to gather a band of armed men. This could be done without any suspicion. As for his part, tomorrow after going to the citadel to worship as usual, he would invite those men to dine with him. Then Amphimachus, along with his band, must rush in and kill them.

Amphimachus agreed to this plan and promised to carry it out. And then he departed from Priam.

|39| During the same day, Antenor, Polydamas, Ucalegon, and Dolon met in secret. They were amazed at the stubbornness of the king, who, when surrounded by the enemy, preferred to die rather than sue for peace, thus causing the destruction of his country and people. Antenor had a plan for solving their problems, and if the others would swear their allegiance, he would reveal it.

When all had sworn as he wished, he first sent word to Aeneas, and then told them his plan. They must, he said, betray their country, and in such a way that they might safeguard themselves and their families. Someone must go—someone that no one could suspect—and tell Agamemnon. They must act quickly. He had noticed that Priam, when leaving the council, was enraged because he had urged him to sue for peace; and he feared that the king was devising some treachery.

All promised their aid and immediately chose Polydamas— he would arouse least suspicion—to go in secret and see Agamemnon.

Thus Polydamas, having gone to the camp of the Greeks, saw Agamemnon and told him the plan.

|40| That night Agamemnon called all the leaders to a secret meeting of the council, and gave them the news, and asked their advice. The council decided unanimously to trust the traitors. As for the plan, Ulysses and Nestor said that they were afraid to carry it out; but Neoptolemus spoke in its favor; and thus a disagreement arose, which it was decided to settle by obtaining a password from Polydamas that Sinon might test with Aeneas, Anchises, and Antenor.

Thus Sinon went to Troy and tested the password (Amphimachus had not yet stationed his guards at the gate), and returned and told Agamemnon that Aeneas, Anchises, and Antenor had given the correct countersign. Then the members of the council, binding themselves on oath, promised that if Troy were betrayed the next night, no harm would come to Antenor, Ucalegon, Polydamas, Aeneas, and Dolon, or to any of their parents, or indeed to their children, wives, relatives, friends, and associates, or to any of their property.

When they had sworn to this promise, Polydamas gave them instructions. At night, he said, they must lead the army to the Scaean gate—the one whose exterior was carved with a horse's head.[32] Antenor and Aeneas would be in charge of the guard at this point, and they would open the bolt and raise a torch as the sign for attack.

|41| Their agreement being complete in every detail, Polydamas

returned to the city and reported the success of his mission. Antenor, Aeneas, and all their associates, he said, must go by night to the Scaean gate and open the bolt, and raise a torch, and thus welcome the Greeks.

That night Antenor and Aeneas were ready at the gate and let Neoptolemus in. After opening the bolt and raising the torch, they looked to a means of escape for themselves and their people.

Antenor, with Neoptolemus providing protection, led the way to the palace, to the point where the Trojans had posted a guard. Then Neoptolemus, breaking into the palace and slaughtering the Trojans, pursued and cut down Priam at the altar of Jupiter.

Hecuba, fleeing with Polyxena, met with Aeneas and entrusted her daughter to him. He had her concealed at the home of his father, Anchises.

Andromache and Cassandra hid in the temple of Minerva.

During the whole night the Greeks did not cease wreaking slaughter and carrying off plunder.

|42| With the coming of day, Agamemnon called all his leaders to a meeting on the citadel. After giving thanks to the gods, he praised the army and ordered that all the booty be gathered together and fairly divided. At the same time he asked them what they wanted to do with Antenor and Aeneas and those who had helped betray Troy. All of them answered, with a loud shout, that they wanted to honor their promise to these.

Thus Agamemnon, having summoned all of the traitors, confirmed them in all of their rights. Antenor, when Agamemnon had granted him leave to speak, began by thanking the Greeks. Then he bade them to remember how Helenus and Cassandra had always pled with Priam for peace, and how Helenus had successfully urged the return of Achilles' body for burial. Accordingly, Agamemnon, following the advice of the council, gave Helenus and Cassandra their freedom.

Then Helenus, remembering how Hecuba and Andromache had always loved him, interceded with Agamemnon in their behalf.

And again Agamemnon, by advice of the council, gave these their freedom.

Then he made an equitable division of the booty and rendered thanks to the gods with the sacrifice of a victim.

The council voted that they should return to their homeland on the fifth day.

|43| When the time for sailing arrived, a great storm arose and raged several days; Calchas informed them that the spirits of the dead were displeased.

Then Neoptolemus, remembering that Polyxena, the cause of his father's death, had not been found in the palace, voiced his complaint; he blamed the army and demanded that Agamemnon produce her.

Agamemnon summoned Antenor and told him to find Polyxena and bring her there.

Accordingly, Antenor went to Aeneas and earnestly begged him to hand over Polyxena, so that the Greeks would set sail. And thus, having found where she had been hidden, he took her to Agamemnon.

And Agamemnon gave her to Neoptolemus.

And Neoptolemus cut her throat at the grave of his father.

Agamemnon was angry with Aeneas for hiding Polyxena and ordered him and his followers to depart from their country immediately. Thus Aeneas and all of his followers departed.

For several days after Agamemnon set sail, Helen, returning home with Menelaus, her husband, was grieved more deeply than when she had come.

Helenus went to the Chersonese, accompanied by Cassandra, his sister, and Andromache, the wife of his brother Hector, and Hecuba, his mother.

|44| So much and no more Dares the Phrygian put into writing, for, as a faithful follower of Antenor, he stayed on at Troy.[33]

The war against Troy lasted ten years, six months, and twelve days.

The number of Greeks who fell, according to the *Journal* that Dares wrote, was 866,000; the number of the Trojans 676,000.

Aeneas set sail with the twenty-two ships that Alexander had used when going to Greece.

He had about 3,400 followers, people of all different ages; Antenor had about 2,500; Andromache and Helenus about 1,200.

BIBLIOGRAPHY

This bibliography lists the latest editions of Dictys and Dares along with some of the most important scholarly books and articles which deal with them and their influence.

EDITIONS

Daretis Phrygii De Excidio Troiae Historia, ed. Ferdinand Meister. Leipzig, 1873.

Dictyis Cretensis Ephemeridos Belli Troiani Libri, ed. Werner Eisenhut. Leipzig, 1958.

SCHOLARSHIP

Greif, Wilhelm. *Die Mittelalterlichen Bearbeitungen der Trojanersage.* Marburg, 1886.

Griffin, Nathaniel Edward. *Dares and Dictys, An Introduction to the Study of Medieval Versions of the Story of Troy.* Baltimore, 1907.

———. "The Greek Dictys," *American Journal of Philology,* XXIX, 3 (1908), 329-335.

———. "Un-Homeric Elements in the Medieval Story of Troy," *The Journal of English and Germanic Philology,* VII (1907-1908), 32-52.

Schissel von Fleschenberg, Otmar. *Dares-Studien.* Halle an-der-Salle, 1908.

Young, Karl. *The Origin and Development of the Story of Troilus and Criseyde,* Chaucer Soc., 2nd Ser., No. 40. London, 1908 [for 1904].

169

NOTES

INTRODUCTION

1. The following Byzantine writers based their stories of the Trojan War on the Greek Dictys: Joannes Malalas (sixth century), Joannes Antiochenos (seventh century), and Georgias Kedrenos (eleventh century). See Nathaniel Edward Griffin, *Dares and Dictys, An Introduction to the Study of Medieval Versions of the Story of Troy* (Baltimore, 1907), pp. 34-108. On the influence of the original Dares on Malalas, see our Introduction, p. 12.

2. This summary is given by Karl Young, *The Origin and Development of the Story of Troilus and Criseyde*, Chaucer Soc., 2nd Ser., No. 40 (London, 1908 [for 1904]), p. 2. Young, p. 2, n. 2, contrasts Dictys' account as follows: Hippodamia, and not Briseida, is the daughter of Brises; there are no equivalents for Dares' portraits; Troilus, who is mentioned only in a passage recording his death, is never connected with the often mentioned Diomedes; Calchas is a Greek priest.

3. These portraits are given in Dares 12 (Troilus) and 13 (Briseida and Diomedes).

4. Dares 31.

5. Dares 15.

6. Guido's work was widely adapted, as, for instance, by John Lydgate in his *Troy-book*. See Wilhelm Greif, *Die Mittelalterlichen Bearbeitungen der Trojanersage* (Marburg, 1886), pp. 64-70.

7. Guido shows some direct knowledge of Dares too. See Greif, pp. 57-64.

8. See R. M. Lumiansky, "The Story of Troilus and Briseida according to Benoit and Guido," *Speculum*, XXIX, 4 (October 1954), 727-733.

9. Young, p. 12.

10. The renaming of Briseida is perhaps due to a confusion of her father, the seer Calchas, with the priest of Apollo, Chryses, the father of Chryseis (in the *Iliad*). Boccaccio may have been influenced to make this change of name by Armannino's *Florita*, which uses "Criseida" instead of "Briseida," and which was composed slightly earlier than the *Filostrato*. See Griffin's Introduction, *The Filostrato of Giovanni Boccaccio*, trans. Nathaniel Edward Griffin and Arthur Beckwith Myrick (Philadelphia, 1929), p. 26, n. 1.

170

11. Pandaro seems to have no other connection than his name with the Pandarus of Lycia mentioned in Dictys and Dares and in the *Iliad*. Griffin, Introduction, pp. 41-42, thinks that Boccaccio used this particular name only because of its fancied etymology: Pandaro is the one who "gives all" to Troilo.

12. Young, pp. 36-55, lists these similarities along with many others.

13. Compare Dictys 3.2-3 and Dares 27.

14. Young, p. 139.

15. Young, p. 105.

16. The French translator of Guido was Raoul le Fèvre. See Alice Walker, ed., *Troilus and Cressida* by Shakespeare (Cambridge, England, 1957), xxxviii-xlvi.

17. See Dictys 1.19 and 6.10.

18. *Aethiopis*, fragment 1 in *Hesiod, the Homeric Hymns, and Homerica*, ed. by Hugh G. Evelyn-White in the Loeb series (London and Cambridge, Mass., 1936), pp. 507-509.

19. Dictys 4.10-11 and Dares 34.

20. See N. E. Griffin, "Un-Homeric Elements in the Story of Troy," *The Journal of English and Germanic Philology*, VII (1907-1908), 32-52.

21. Griffin, "Un-Homeric Elements," p. 37.

22. Werner Eisenhut, ed. *Dictyis Cretensis Ephemeridos Belli Troiani Libri* (Teubner, Leipzig, 1958), p. xii (praefatio).

23. These claims are discussed by Nathaniel E. Griffin, "The Greek Dictys," *American Journal of Philology*, XXIX (1908), 331.

24. *The Tebtunis Papyri*, ed. Grenfell-Hunt-Goodspeed, Part II (London, 1907), pp. 9 ff. The Dictys-fragment is also edited by Eisenhut, pp. 134-139. The fragment covers Dictys 4.8 (end)-4.15 (middle).

25. Which may be translated: "No small grief came upon the Trojans when Troilus died, for he was still young and noble and handsome."

The brackets indicate a blank in the papyrus; the word ὡραῖος has been supplied from Malalas, a Byzantine writer whose Troy story depends on the Greek Dictys, and on the basis of the Latin translation, *forma corporis*. See Griffin, *AJP*, 331, note 2.

26. See our text (the last sentence of Dictys 4.9) for a translation.

27. Hermann Dunger, "Dictys-Septimius: Über die unsprüngliche

Abfassung und die Quellen der Ephemeris Belli Troiani," *Programm des Vitzhumschens Gymnasiums* (Dresden, 1878), p. 7.

28. Henrich Pratje, *Quaestiones Sallustianae ad Lucium Septimium et Sulpicium Severum Gai Sallusti Crispi imitatores spectantes* (Göttingen, 1874).

29. Griffin, *AJP*, 331, who cites Pratje, p. 10. The reference to Sallust is *Bellum Jugurthinum* 7.1.

30. Malalas *Chronographia* 5. See Griffin, *AJP*, 334-335.

31. These sources are Eudokia and Suidas. See note 7 to the Letter and note 3 to the Preface.

32. Léopold Constans, ed. *Le Roman de Troie par Benoit de Sainte-Maure*, Vol. VI, Société des Anciens Textes Français (Paris, 1912), pp. 196-197.

33. Constans, pp. 196-197.

34. Other discrepancies are pointed out in the notes to the Dictys-Letter.

35. Nathaniel E. Griffin, *Dares and Dictys* (Baltimore, 1907), pp. 118-120.

36. *Papyri*, p. 10.

37. Griffin, *AJP*, 335.

38. Titus 1.12-13 (King James Version).

39. Plutarch *Caesar* 22. See Eisenhut, p. vi (praefatio).

40. Otmar Schissel von Fleschenberg, *Dares Studien* (Halle ander-Salle, 1908), pp. 84-85.

41. The reference of Ptolemy Chennos is found in Photius *Bibliotheca*, cod. 190, p. 147 (Bekker).

42. Schissel von Fleschenberg, pp. 84-157.

43. Dracontius *Romulea* 8. See Schissel von Fleschenberg, p. 169.

44. *Mythographus Vaticanus Primus* 24. See Schissel von Fleschenberg, p. 169.

45. Schissel von Fleschenberg, pp. 84-96.

46. Schissel von Fleschenberg, pp. 89-90.

47. Schissel von Fleschenberg, pp. 89-90.

48. Schissel von Fleschenberg, pp. 160-169. For the exceptions, see notes 9, 10, 11, 12, 13, 17, and 31 to Dares.

49. Schissel von Fleschenberg, p. 91.

50. Gilbert Highet, *The Classical Tradition: Greek and Roman Influences on Western Literature*, third printing with corrections (Oxford, 1953), p. 51.

51. *Ephemeridos Belli Troiani Libri.*

52. *Daretis Phrygii De Excidio Troiae Historia,* ed. Ferdinand Meister (Teubner, Leipzig, 1873).

53. Unpubl. thesis (Univ. of Texas, 1959) by William Huie Hess, "Dictys the Cretan, Journal of the Trojan War, A Translation."

54. Dares Phrygius, *The faythfull and true storye of the Destruction of Troy,* trans. Thomas Paynell (London, 1553). This translation has not been seen; according to Clarissa P. Farrar and Austin P. Evans, *Bibliography of English Translations from Medieval Sources* (Columbia Univ. Press, 1946), p. 148, it "appears to exist only in a unique copy in the Bodleian Library."

55. Dares Phrygius, *The History of the Fall of Troy,* trans. Margaret Schlauch, in *Medieval Narrative, A Book of Translations* (New York, 1928, pp. 247-279. The Delphin edition is *Dictys Cretensis et Dares Phrygius De Bello Trojano ex editione Samuelis Artopoei,* pub. with notes of previous scholars by A. J. Valpy (London, 1825). This edition, as its title page indicates, is based on that of Samuel Artopoeus (Strasbourg, 1691).

DICTYS

LETTER

1. For a discussion of problems concerning the Letter and the Preface, see Introduction, pp. 7-10.

2. The Preface names only Cadmus. Dictys 5.17 names Cadmus and Danaus; here we must suppose that the author of the Letter has forgotten his own translation.

3. In the Preface an earthquake lays open the tomb.

4. Praxis is the Eupraxides of the Preface.

5. In the Preface the language is Phoenician instead of Greek.

6. In the Preface Eupraxides gives the books to Rutilius Rufus, the governor of Crete, and Rufus sees that they get to Nero.

7. The manuscripts, all of which give the number of abridged books as five, have been corrected to agree with the reports of Eudokia and Suidas that the total number of books was nine. See Preface, note 3.

PREFACE

1. The Atridae are Agamemnon and Menelaus, who, however, in Dictys, are not the real sons of Atreus, but of Plisthenes. See Dictys 1.1.

2. Achaea is the Roman province of Greece.

3. The manuscripts, all of which give the total number of books as six, have been corrected to agree with the reports of Eudokia and Suidas. See Letter, note 7.

4. This sentence might also be translated: "Rufus . . . sent them to Nero along with Eupraxides himself."

BOOK 1

1. Atreus is apparently identified with Catreus, who was the son of Minos (Apollodorus 3.1.2).

2. Agamemnon and Menelaus are the sons of Plisthenes in Hesiod *The Catalogues of Women* (fragment 69, p. 203, ed. Evelyn-White).

3. Dictys always uses "Alexander" instead of "Paris." "Phrygian" is a synonym for "Trojan."

4. In the *Cypria* (fragment 1, p. 491, ed. Evelyn-White), Iris is the one who brings this news.

5. According to Malalas (*Chronographia* 5.118-119), Aethra persuaded Helen to yield to Alexander. In the *Cypria* (fragment 1, p. 491), Venus brings Helen and Alexander together.

6. Apparently Pelops was the great hero of the past from whom aristocratic families liked to claim descent, and often did so falsely.

7. This embassy appears before the Trojan council in Dictys 1.6 and before the Trojan assembly in Dictys 1.10(middle)-11. It should be compared with the later, similar embassy in Dictys 2.20-26.

8. Ilus had led an army against Pelops and chased him out of Lydia. See Pausanias *Description of Greece* 2.2.24.

9. Danaus and Agenor were related as follows: Neptune was the father of Belus and Agenor by Libya, and Belus was the father of Danaus. See Apollod. 2.1.4.

10. The text, which reads "Plesione" here, has been corrected to "Hesione," to agree with Dictys 4.22, where the same genealogy is given.

11. Admetus' wife was Alcestis. See Euripides *Alcestis*.

12. See Sophocles *Trachiniae*.

13. Section 17, with a few exceptions, is based on Homer's catalogue of ships in *Iliad* 2.494-795.

14. The text is corrupt here. This Phalis is probably to be equated

with the Phalas of Dictys 4.4.

15. Perhaps Agamemnon had consulted the oracle of Apollo, and this woman is Apollo's priestess, the Pythia.

16. In the *Cypria* (fragment 1, p. 495), Diana snatches Iphigenia away and carries her off to the land of the Taurians.

17. Anius was a king of Delos. For him and his daughters, see Ovid *Metamorphoses* 13.631-673.

BOOK 2

1. Diomedes' father, Tydeus, had helped Polynices gather an army for the attack against Thebes. See *Iliad* 4.376-379.

2. Telephus, whose real father was Hercules, was, according to Apollod. 3.9.1, Teuthras' adopted son. Compare Dares 16.

3. According to Euripides (*Heraclidae* 210-211), Hercules' mother, Alcmene, was the daughter of Pelops.

4. According to Euripides (*Iphigenia in Aulis* 94-414), Menelaus persuaded Agamemnon to sacrifice Iphigenia, and prevented him from countermanding the letter by which she had been summoned to Aulis.

5. This section provides two different guides for the Greeks: the Scythians and Telephus. Furthermore, the part about Telephus seems inconsistent with earlier sections. Previously Telephus had refused to help the Greeks because of his relationship with Priam (Dictys 2.5); and Machaon and Podalirius had already bound his wound (Dictys 2.6).

6. Dictys differs from all other accounts of how Palamedes was slain. For instance, in the *Cypria* (fragment 19, p. 505), Palamedes is drowned—he had gone out fishing—by Diomedes and Ulysses.

7. This Teuthras is not to be confused with the father of Teuthranius (Dictys 2.3).

8. This embassy (Dictys 2.20-26) is the one to which Homer refers: Ulysses makes the main speech (compare *Iliad* 3.204-224), and Antimachus urges that Menelaus should not be allowed to return to the Greek camp (compare *Iliad* 11.122-142). In the earlier embassy Palamedes made the main speech. See Dictys 1.4 (end), 6, and 10 (middle)-11.

9. The daughter of Menelaus and Helen is Hermione (Dictys 6.4).

10. Sections 2.28-4.1 cover the events described in the *Iliad*.

11. This list is taken for the most part from Homer's catalogue of Trojan allies in *Iliad* 2.824-877.

12. The text, which is corrupt here, has been emended to agree with *Iliad* 2.842-843.

13. There is a lacuna in the text beween "Acamas" and "Pirus."

14. According to Aristotle (*Rhetoric* 2.24), Achilles was terribly angry with the Greeks on Tenedos because he had not been invited to dinner.

15. According to Euripides (*Rhesus* 41-146), Hector sent Dolon to find out why the Greeks had lit their fires and gathered, in an uproar, around Agamemnon's hut. Compare *Iliad* 10.

16. How different is this Achilles from the Achilles of *Iliad* 9!

17. The temple of the Thymbraean Apollo was located in a grove east of Troy where the Thymbrius River emtpied into the Scamander. See Strabo *Geography* 13.1.35.

BOOK 3

1. For Phineus' relationship with Priam, see Dictys 4.22.

2. Penthesilea does not arrive until Dictys 4.2.

3. Sections 17-19, which describe the funeral games in honor of Patroclus, should be compared with *Iliad* 23.

4. Sections 20-27, which describe the ransoming of Hector's body, should be compared with *Iliad* 24.

5. Helen's god-like brothers were Castor and Pollux. See *Iliad* 3.236-242.

BOOK 4

1. The tomb of Ilus is mentioned in *Iliad* 10.415 and 11.372.

2. See Dictys 1.5.

3. The spelling of this name is doubtful.

4. In the *Aethiopis* (fragment 1, p. 507, ed. Evelyn-White), Aurora obtains immortality for her son from Jupiter.

5. Sigeum was located at the mouth of the Scamander River. Strabo tells of a temple and a monument of Achilles in this area, and also of monuments of Patroclus and Antilochus. See his *Geography* 13.1.31-32.

6. See Dictys 2.10 and 12.

7. See Sophocles *Philoctetes*.

8. See Dictys 2.23-24. In the *Iliad* (11.122-162), Agamemnon slaughters the two sons of Antimachus because their father had

opposed the return of Helen and had plotted the death of Menelaus.

9. See Dictys 1.9 and note 8 thereto.

BOOK 5

1. The spelling of this name is doubtful.

2. Compare Panthus' conciliatory remarks in Dictys 2.23 and 2.25.

3. Theano is mentioned in *Iliad* 5.70 as the wife of Antenor and in *Iliad* 6.302 as the priestess of Minerva.

4. See *Iliad* 7.452-453.

5. In other accounts the armor of Achilles is the object of contention.

6. Rhoeteum is north of Sigeum. Strabo tells of a tomb and temple of Ajax on the shore nearby. See his *Geography* 13.1.30.

BOOK 6

1. Sections 5 and 6 cover the events of the *Odyssey*.

2. According to Dictys 2.43 (end), Mestor was slain at Troy.

3. Compare Dictys 4.4, where Memnon's forces slay their leader Phalas (not Pallas) and choose to stay on Rhodes (not Paphos).

4. Aurora (Dawn) is the mother of Himera (Longing)-Hemera (Day).

5. Compare Dictys 5.16, where Neoptolemus gives the sons of Hector to Helenus.

6. Compare the prophecy of Tiresias in *Odyssey* 11.134-137: "Death will come to you out of the sea...."

7. Telegonus is the son of the mortal Ulysses and the immortal Circe.

DARES

[LETTER]

1. The brackets indicate that the heading has been supplied, without any manuscript support, for the purpose of easy reference. For a discussion of problems concerning the letter, see Introduction, pp. 11-14.

SECTIONS 1-44

1. But Pelias ruled in Thessaly, not in the Peloponnese.

2. There is an *Argonautica* attributed to Orpheus which, how-

ever, is dependent upon Apollonius Rhodius. Orpheus was one of the Argonauts.

3. Perhaps this army was fighting the Amazons. See *Iliad* 3.182-190.

4. Peleus was Telamon's brother.

5. The compiler, who is here basing his work upon Dracontius, has substituted "Diana" for "Dione," which is the reading of Dracontius *Romulea* 8.435. Dione, of whom apparently the compiler had never heard, was, according to *Iliad* 5.370, the mother of Venus. See Schissel von Fleschenberg, pp. 154-156.

6. This name does not appear in Dracontius, who is the source for this passage. Accordingly, "Helaea," which is probably to be derived from "Helen," must have been added later either by the compiler or someone else. See Schissel von Fleschenberg, p. 156.

7. The compiler, having already substituted Diana for Dione, now adds Diana's brother, Apollo. See note 5 above.

8. Schissel von Fleschenberg (pp. 147 ff.) thinks that this sentence begins the translation of the original Dares somewhere in the middle of its introduction, a large part of which has been replaced by the material in sections 1 through 10.

9. Sections 1 through 10 give the capture of Hesione, and the failure of Antenor's mission to seek her recovery, as the cause of the War, whereas the original Dares, as shown in sections 11 through 43, blame the War on Helen's abduction. Accordingly, references to Hesione and to Antenor's mission in sections 11 through 43 are probably additions of the translator-compiler for the purpose of harmonizing his different sources. See Schissel von Fleschenberg, p. 147.

10. Schissel von Fleschenberg (pp. 9-12, and 147) thinks that references to Castor and Pollux in sections 11 and 12 are additions of the translator-compiler for the purpose of connecting his Dares-translation with the earlier sections, in which Castor and Pollux play important roles.

11. According to Schissel von Fleschenberg, this sentence probably belongs to an original Greek Preface. See Introduction, pp. 13-14.

12. See note 10 above.

13. Helen, as well as her brothers, is perhaps out of place here. See note 10 above.

14. This list is for the most part based on Homer's catalogue of ships in *Iliad* 2.494-759.

15. Compare Dictys 2.10 and note 5 thereto.

16. Compare this section with Dictys 2.1-6 and note 2 thereto.

17. According to Schissel von Fleschenberg, most of this speech is probably the work of the translator-compiler. See note 9 above.

18. This catalogue of Trojan allies is based for the most part on *Iliad* 2.824-877.

19. Schissel von Fleschenberg (p. 162) points out that the non-Homeric hero Palamedes (with his ships) is not listed in section 14 along with the other Greek leaders (and their ships) but is given a special place here after the listing of the Trojan leaders.

20. For Anius, compare Dictys 1.23 (end) and note 16 thereto.

21. According to Dictys (2.11), Aeneas slew Protestilaus.

22. Compare *Iliad* 7, where Hector and Ajax, after their duel, exchange gifts and part in friendship.

23. There are eleven truces reported in Dares, lasting, all told, more than seven and a half years.

24. Compare *Iliad* 1.1-4, in which the Wrath of Achilles hurls many brave souls of heroes to Hades.

25. Compare the duel between Alexander and Menelaus in *Iliad* 3, where Venus rescues Alexander out of the battle; and in Dictys 2.40, where the barbarians rescue him. Notice that Dares has Alexander (and not Pandarus, as in Homer and Dictys) wound Menelaus with an arrow.

26. Compare Dictys 2.3 (end) and Dares 39 (beginning).

27. Compare Dictys 4.15, where Ajax sees to the building of a tomb for Achilles.

28. Compare the different account in Dictys 5.15.

29. Compare the different account in Dictys 4.3.

30. Apparently Dares has created the character of Amphimachus after that of Antimachus in the traditional account. Compare Dictys 2.23-24 and 4.21.

31. According to Schissel von Fleschenberg, Priam's speech is, up to this point, probably the work of the translator-compiler. See note 9 above.

32. Thus Dares explains the wooden horse away.

33. According to Schissel von Fleschenberg, this section is probably based on an original Greek Preface. See Introduction, pp. 13-14.

INDEX OF PROPER NAMES

This index is based on the English translation. Its preparation, however, was facilitated by the use of the indexes of Eisenhut and Meister to their Latin editions. References are to page numbers: 19-130 refer to Dictys, 133-168 to Dares.